Explorers

written by
Elizabeth Koehler-Pentacoff

illustrated by
Wayne Reid

© Frank Schaffer Publications, Inc. FS10131 Explorers

FS-10131 Explorers
All rights reserved–Printed in the U.S.A.
Copyright © 1994 Frank Schaffer Publications, Inc.
23740 Hawthorne Blvd.
Torrance, CA 90505

Table of Contents

Introduction

Each unit of *Explorers* begins with a narration set in the past allowing students to relive the exploration. Suggested teaching strategies follow the text as well as a bibliography for student reading. The strategies include activities for writing, art, science, and history. Every explorer unit contains a page of multiple choice questions to determine student comprehension of what they have read. This page can also be used for unit review. Each section contains activities to encourage further research. The book concludes with the Explorers Trivia Game, a fun way for the entire class to review the material.

Meriwether **Lewis** and William **Clark**

On April 30, 1803, France and the United States signed the Louisiana Purchase agreement. Napoleon had sold France's Louisiana Territory to the United States for 15 million dollars. At 827,987 square miles, this purchase doubled the area of the United States. Since the United States only paid about four cents an acre, the land was the bargain of the century.

The President wanted to learn about the region's geography, plants, animals, and native American cultures. He hoped to become friends with the Indians that lived there. The Sioux Indians had been allies of the British during the Revolutionary War and had disliked Americans. Jefferson hoped to foster a better relationship with them and other tribes. He also realized that America's economy would be improved by finding new sources of furs and a water route to transport them.

Consequently, President Jefferson asked Congress for money to fund the trip. His request for $25,000 was granted. Meriwether Lewis and William Clark led the expedition across the western United States. The commanding officer, 28-year-old Meriwether Lewis, had been the president's secretary. Lewis' interest in plants and animals would be helpful in making observations and gathering data. Lewis chose his friend, 33-year-old William Clark, to accompany him. Clark had been his commanding officer in the army.

A crew of 50 journeyed on this exploration. Seaman, Lewis' large dog traveled with them acting as both hunter and protector. At one point the Chinook Indians tried to steal Seaman from Lewis. Before the crew began the journey, they constructed a keelboat with sails, bought two canoes, and packed supplies. Besides clothing, blankets, tools, medicine, weapons, and scientific instruments, they brought medals, flags, and certificates for the Indians.

Because Indians thought flags had magical powers, peace medals were placed on ribbons so the Indians could wear them around their necks. Many times the Indians continued to wear them after death, because these medals were so highly cherished.

In exchange for these medals, the Indians would be loyal to the United States. Since Britain and Spain also wanted friendship of the tribes, loyalty was considered very important.

On May 14, 1804, the exploring party left Camp Wood. Lewis and Clark brought along René Jusseaume, a French-Canadian trader, who would be an advisor and interpreter. He had lived with the Mandan Indians and was married to a Mandan woman.

Toussaint Charbonneau, another trader, also joined the group. He had lived with the Hidatsas. One of his wives, Sacagawea, a Shoshoni Indian, also came along. She was only 16 years old and pregnant, but she proved to be a very valuable addition to the crew. Besides guiding them through the wilderness, she gathered wild foods that no one else could find and served as an interpreter and ambassadress to the Indian tribes. She was instrumental in convincing tribes that the party needed to barter for horses. Without her, the explorers may have never succeeded in their mission.

Pushing poles in the water, the crew moved the keelboat up the Missouri River. In September they met the Sioux Indians. The Sioux were not happy with the gifts they were given and tensions grew. The Indians performed a scalp dance, showing enemy scalps on sticks, and dancers pantomimed their fighting skills. One of the Sioux chiefs wanted war. However, Chief Black Buffalo made certain that the visitors were able to leave peacefully.

In October Lewis and Clark's party met the Arikaras. The Indians were impressed with Clark's slave, York, since they had never seen a black man before.

Winter arrived so the explorers built Fort Mandan, near the Mandan and Hidatsa tribes. (This location is near what is now Bismarck, North Dakota.) Sacagawea's baby, Jean Baptiste (Pomp), was born here. One recorded temperature in Fort Mandan was -54°. Lewis set some liquor outside as an experiment. Fifteen minutes later it was ice!

On April 7, 1805, some of the crew members took the keelboat back to St. Louis. They took with them live animals (four magpies, one prairie dog, and a grouse), animal skins, skeletons, specimens of soil and plants, Indian bows and arrows, and a Mandan language dictionary. President Jefferson and scientists would learn many things about the newly explored territory.

The rest of the explorers continued up the Missouri River. Winds, strong currents, and rapids made progress difficult.

Where they stopped to camp, a grizzly bear charged them, and one man had to jump in the river to escape. Another bear treed a man. The man had to stay in the tree all day until the bear finally left in the evening.

The party carried its boats and supplies for 18 miles until it came to waterfalls. They built makeshift wagons and traveled over steep, rocky inclines. When the explorers passed the falls, they traveled once again by boat making camp where the river branched into three forks.

Then the group met the Shoshoni Indians. Sacagawea was surprised and happy to find her brother. He was the Shoshoni Indian chief. On what is now the Idaho/Montana border, the group crossed the Bitterroot Mountain Range, forging a way on sheer, rocky slopes. It became so cold their moccasins froze stiff! Since food was scarce, the explorers were forced to kill and eat some of their horses. They even consumed candles.

Finally, the party came to a valley where the Nez Perce Indians gave them food and maps. The Indians promised to keep their horses until the group returned. The explorers made canoes by burning out logs and used them on the Clearwater, Snake, and Columbia rivers. They overturned many times due to the very rough waters.

Lewis, Clark, and their party met the Wanapam Indians who were head-flatteners. They pressed the babies' heads between boards to flatten the front of the skull, nose, and forehead. The Indians thought this made them beautiful. The explorers were horrified.

In November 1805, Lewis and Clark reached the coast. They built Fort Clatsop (near what is now Astoria, Oregon) and spent the winter there. During this time they suffered from illnesses and from the effects of numerous fleas.

To get ready for their journey home, the group made clothes, moccasins, maps, and wrote in their journals. Lewis described the Indians and their cultures and wrote about plants and animals that were new to him.

On March 23, 1806, the explorers started home. When they went back to the Nez Perce Indians to retrieve their horses, Clark practiced medicine in return for dogs. The crew liked to eat dog meat as they claimed it tasted good and was healthy for them. Many Indians looked down upon them for this.

On July 3 the explorers split into two groups. Lewis and his crew took a shorter route through the mountains. Clark's group explored the Yellowstone River.

Lewis met the Blackfeet Indians. He made a big mistake by telling these warriors of his friendship with the Nez Perces and the Shoshonis. He did not realize the Blackfeet Indians considered these tribes enemies.

That night Indians took some of the crew's guns. In the scuffle one of Lewis's men stabbed one of the Indians in the heart. When the Indians tried to steal their horses, Lewis shot and killed another Indian. The other warriors ran away.

Shortly after this occurrence, one of Lewis' party accidentally shot Lewis in his backside! The man had thought that Lewis, dressed in buckskin, was an elk!

Both Lewis and Clark reunited at the Missouri River in August. Lewis, still recuperating from his injury, turned command of the expedition over to Clark. The group arrived in St. Louis, amidst cheers, on Sept 23, 1806, after traveling 8,000 miles.

▶ Suggested Teaching Strategies

Students can further research the Lewis and Clark expedition using sources such as *The Incredible Journey of Lewis and Clark* by Rhoda Blumberg (Lothrop, Lee, and Shepard), *Sacajawea* by Harold P. Howard (University of Oklahoma Press), and *The Journals of Lewis and Clark* (Tirres Mirror Publishers).

1. Have each student choose a plant or animal that Lewis and Clark discovered and create a science project about it. Example: Where is the plant found? Do we have a use for it today? Sketch the plant. Grow it. Where does the animal live? Build a model of the type of home it inhabits.

2. Have the class pretend that Lewis and Clark never made their trip and Napoleon never sold the Louisiana Purchase to the United States. Students may rewrite history as to what could have happened and how it might have affected us today.

3. Have students paint landscapes of what Lewis and Clark saw. Examples: Buffalo herds, the plains, an Indian ceremony. . . .

4. As a class, act out a scene when Captain Lewis gave his "Great Father" speech to the Indians. Students may create dialog containing things he might have said.

5. Students may make a map and trace the area of the Louisiana Purchase.

6. Students may write poems about one of their experiences. It can be about an Indian tribe, how the explorers suffered, or the beauty of the land they explored.

7. Students may make a model of one of the following:
   a. one of the boats Lewis and Clark used
   b. a fort they made
   c. an Indian village they saw

8. Write a legend told by an Indian who met Lewis and Clark.

9. How did Lewis and Clark treat medical problems? Have students do research and compare Lewis and Clark's treatment to today's treatments.

10. Study the early 1800s. What was going on in the rest of the world at that time? Students may make a scrapbook of clippings, drawings, and short articles about recreation, the economy, politics, world events, and life styles of the time.

Name _____

THE TRAIL

After reading the article, circle the correct answer.

1. The Wanapam Indians
   a. were warrior Indians that fought with the explorer's crew.
   b. were head-flatteners.
   c. pierced their noses with rings and bones.

2. Sacagawea was a
   a. Chinook Indian.
   b. Mandan Indian.
   c. Shoshoni Indian.

3. Lewis and Clark left Camp Wood on
   a. April 17, 1805.
   b. May 14, 1804.
   c. April 30, 1803.

4. When food became scarce, the explorers had to eat
   a. their horses and candles.
   b. the sails of their keelboat.
   c. plants that made them ill.

5. Throughout the journey Lewis and Clark's crew was forced to kill _____ Indians.
   a. 10
   b. 56
   c. 2

6. William Clark doctored the Indians in exchange for
   a. dogs to eat.
   b. horses to ride.
   c. bow and arrows for protection.

7. The crew traveled a total of
   a. 8,000 miles.
   b. 12,000 miles.
   c. 4,000 miles.

8. Lewis had an accident after the fight with the Blackfeet Indians.
   a. He was shot with a bow and arrow by an Indian.
   b. He was bitten by a snake.
   c. He was shot with a gun by one of his crew.

Name _____

FRONTIER FOLKS

Place the letter of the name of the person in the blank beside the description below that best describes him or her.

_____ 1. Clark's slave nicknamed "The Big Medicine" by Arikaras. (*Medicine* meant power.)

_____ 2. _____ Indians gave the explorers horses to travel in the mountains.

_____ 3. She served as an interpreter and guide for Lewis and Clark.

_____ 4. Secretary of State during Jefferson's administration

_____ 5. Emperor of France

_____ 6. Canadian trader and husband to Sacagawea

_____ 7. He was Jefferson's secretary and then became leader of the expedition

_____ 8. Commander over Lewis in the army

_____ 9. These Indian warriors fought with Lewis and his men.

_____10. Sacagawea's child

    a. Sacagawea
    b. York
    c. Jean Baptiste
    d. Blackfeet Indians
    e. James Madison
    f. Shoshoni
    g. Lewis
    h. Charbonneau
    i. Clark
    j. Napoleon

LEWIS AND CLARK

TRIBES ALONG THE TRAIL

Research and answer the following questions about Indian tribes.

1. In 1876 which famous colonel fought against the Sioux Indians?

   _____

2. Describe homes built by the Arikara Indians.

   _____

3. How did the Shoshoni help Lewis and Clark's expedition?

   _____

4. The Wanapam Indians were head-flatteners. How was this done? Why?

   _____

5. The Chinook Indians tried to steal _____ from Lewis and Clark.

6. Why was the Nez Perce tribe given this name? What does it mean?

   _____

7. Where did the Mandan tribe live?

   _____

Name _____

THE TRAIL TO THE WEST

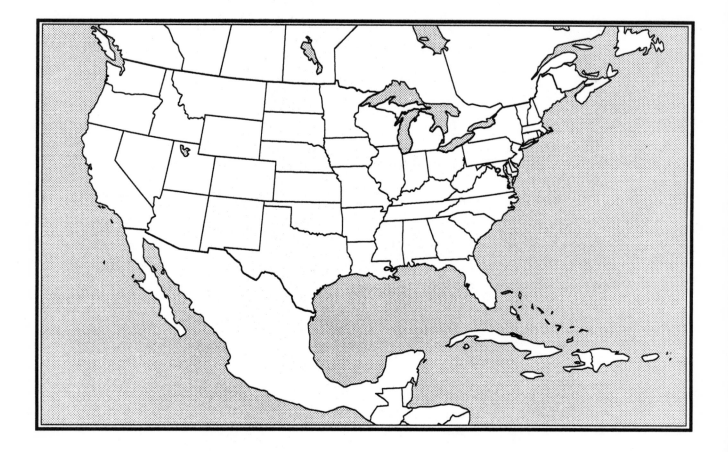

1 Draw the journey of Lewis and Clark. Create a key to show the routes east and west.
2. Outline the area of the Louisiana Purchase.
3. Label the states to the east of this purchase that were already states in 1803.

LEWIS AND CLARK

TIME TRAVEL

This is a time line of events that occurred while Lewis and Clark were exploring. Create newspaper articles about three of the events.

1803 Ohio became the seventeenth state.
      First tax supported public library was founded in Connecticut.
1804 Twelfth Amendment was ratified.
      Vice-President Aaron Burr killed Alexander Hamilton in a duel.
      Oliver Evans built what may have been the first automobile.
1805 Thomas Jefferson began his second term as president.
      The Tripolitan War began.
1806 Zebulon Pike explored the southwestern United States.

Write a biography on one of the people mentioned above. Then create a script of an interview with that person. Perform it with a partner in class.

_____

_____

_____

_____

_____

_____

_____

_____

_____

_____

_____

_____

_____

_____

_____

_____

David Livingstone

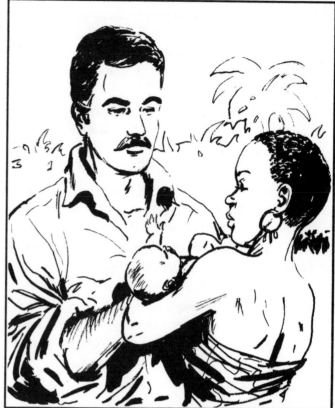

In the 1800s no one knew much about Africa. Called "The Dark Continent," the coast was the only explored region because the Nile, Niger, and Congo rivers were difficult for ships to navigate. The London Missionary Society sent Doctor David Livingstone to Africa to stop the slave trade and to bring Christianity to the Africans.

Livingstone sailed from Britain to South Africa in 1841. The London Missionary Society's station in Kuruman was a big disappointment to him. The missionary's founder, Robert Moffat, had said there were many villages that could use Livingstone's help. But when Livingstone arrived, he found only one small village. Since he really was not needed there, he decided to explore and make his knowledge available to the world. He wanted others to use the rivers as water routes, so traders, doctors, and missionaries could help Africa's economy and people.

He traveled up and down the Zambezi River, across the Kalahari Desert, and he discovered the Victoria Falls. His letters describing his experiences were published in newspapers and magazines. Great Britain considered him a hero.

In February of 1844, while Livingstone was working on a new mission in Mabotsa, he nearly died in a lion attack. A lion had been killing the villagers' sheep, so he shot it. However, the shots only wounded the animal; the lion pushed Livingstone down, grabbed him by the upper left arm, and shook him violently. Natives distracted the beast and saved Livingstone's life. Livingstone had time to reload his gun to kill the lion. Afterwards, he had to set his broken arm himself.

David Livingstone married Robert Moffat's daughter, Mary, in 1845. During their married lives they moved from one mission to another. Mary had five children in six years but still ran schools at the missions.

In 1851 Livingstone left his family in a camp on the Chobe River. He traveled with a companion, William Cotton Oswell, and found the upper Zambezi River. This discovery proved that Central Africa was not merely a desert, but fertile land with several rivers.

His family sailed to England in 1852. He would not see them for five years.

From 1853 to 1856 he made the first crossing of Africa from coast to coast. This successful journey opened a route from the Atlantic Ocean to the Indian Ocean through Africa's interior. Livingstone traveled 4,000 miles of unexplored territory (now known as Angola, Zambia, and Mozambique). His companions on the trip were people of the Makololo tribe. His journey was hampered by his malaria, a sickness caused by mosquito bites.

From the upper Zambezi he traveled until he reached Luanda in May of 1854. He stayed nearly four months there and wrote letters and reports of his journey to the London Missionary Society and the Royal Geographical Society.

In September he started another journey to return to the upper Zambezi to follow it to the Indian Ocean. He found swarming tsetse flies on the Angola River. These insects transmit disease to people.

He was in awe of the waterfalls he saw on November 17, 1855. He named them Victoria Falls, after the queen of Great Britain, Queen Victoria. After six months of following the Zambezi, he reached the Indian Ocean at Quelimane. He thought his travels proved that the Zambezi was a great water route, but he did not realize he had taken a shortcut over the land. In doing so, he missed the Kebrabasa Rapids which were so steep and fast, boats would not be able to pass through them.

In July 1856, Livingstone went home to Great Britain for the first time in 16 years. He had become a national hero. He made speeches across the country and wrote *Missionary Travels and Researches in South Africa*. But he was uncomfortable with his role as "hero" to the public. He just wanted to help the Africans, not to become a celebrity. As Consul for the Portuguese East African Coast, Livingstone did help the country's economic interests.

In 1858 Livingstone began a trip up the Zambezi. His brother, Charles, and a team of Europeans came along, and he argued with them. To make matters worse, they were not able to travel on the Kebrabasa Rapids. However, they did explore Lake Shirwa, Lake Malombe, and Lake Malawi (formerly Lake Nyasa). Mary Livingstone, who was with them, died from malaria in 1862.

Livingstone encountered opposition in abolishing the slave trade. The authorities of Portuguese Mozambique captured slaves and held them with wooden neck yokes. Livingstone fought battles to free the slaves, so the Portuguese complained to the British government. In 1863 the British government recalled the expedition.

Except for his actions against slave traders, he was known as the most peaceful explorer in Africa. He felt slave trading was wrong, so he did not want to leave his steamboat, *Lady Nyasa,* because the slave traders might use it. He sailed the boat across the Indian Ocean to sell it in Bombay. After 46 days and over 2,000 miles of terrible weather, he completed his dangerous journey.

He stayed in London for a year and returned to Africa in 1865. While in Africa, he became ill. His medicine chest was stolen, so he did not have the supplies and drugs to treat himself. Meanwhile, no one in Great Britain had heard from him. People back home were worried.

In 1869 the *New York Herald Newspaper* hired a reporter, Henry Morton Stanley, to find Livingstone. Stanley was successful. In 1871, on the shores of Lake Tanganyika, he met the famous explorer. Stanley's words, "Dr. Livingstone, I presume?" are well-known even today.

Fortunately, Stanley brought medical supplies which saved Livingstone's life. For three months the two explored Lake Tanganyika. Then Stanley took Livingstone's journals back to London. Livingstone's last discovery, Lake Bangweulu, came before his outbreak of dysentery, a painful bowel disease. Livingstone died in April 1873.

His published volumes of letters and journals are the most complete records we have of an African explorer from the nineteenth century.

▶ *Suggested Teaching Strategies*

Students can read more about Livingstone and Africa. Other sources include *The Travels of Livingstone* by Richard Humble (Franklin Watts), *Africa and Its Explorers* by Robert I. Rotberg (Harvard University Press), and *Understanding Africa* by E. Jefferson Murphy (Thomas Crowell).

1. Divide students into groups. Each group may choose a country to study. Each student will:
   a. draw a map of the country and locate latitude, longitude, cities, rivers, mountains, and deserts.
   b. make a model showing the topography of the country.
   c. create a chart comparing our government with that of the country being studied.
   d. design a travel poster advertising the country's positive attributes.
   e. perform a reading or a play about the history of the country.
   f. present material to the class.
   A game may be played to quiz the presenting group. The class asks them 10 questions about the country's geography, economy, people's life styles, and culture. The group is awarded one point for each question answered. One point is subtracted if group members can- not answer the question.

   Sample questions may be created ahead of time and remain the same for all groups. (Sample questions: What crops are grown in the country? What countries border the country? What are the country's natural resources?)

2. Ancient Egypt was one of the world's first civilizations. Have students read about this culture and its written communication. Then students can make up their own hieroglyphic codes.

After they write messages, have them give their messages (along with keys) to friends to decipher.

3. Have students pretend they are television reporters presenting newscasts on "The Rosetta Stone: What Is Its secret?"

4. The class may act out the scene in which Stanley finds Livingstone.

5. Students may read about burial beliefs of the Egyptians. Then they make a model of a pyramid, an obelisk, or a sphinx.

6. Read an African folktale out loud to the class. Students use their own words to write an adaptation of the story. Have them illustrate it with paints, pencils, or a paper collage.

7. The class may paint a mural of costumes and ways of life of the various tribes in Africa that Livingstone may have met.

8. Divide the class into two teams and play "Where in Africa?" Using a large map of Africa, ask one member of a team to point to a location that Livingstone explored. If the person correctly identifies the place within 30 seconds, that team gets one point. The next question goes to the opposing team, or if the first question has been incorrectly answered, the opposing team gets a chance to answer it as well as a new question.

Name _____

LIVINGSTONE'S LIFE

After reading the article about David Livingstone, circle the correct answer.

1. Africa was called
    a. the Unknown Continent.
    b. the Dark Continent.
    c. the Hidden Continent.

2. In 1844 Livingstone almost died when
    a. a lion attacked him.
    b. he caught dysentery.
    c. a mosquito bit him and he came down with malaria.

3. When he crossed Africa, he traveled _____miles of unexplored territory.
    a. 11,000
    b. 8,000
    c. 4,000

4. Livingstone fought with the _____to stop the African slave trade.
    a. Makololo Tribe
    b. Portuguese
    c. British

5. Livingstone took his steamboat and
    a. gave it to a local African tribe.
    b. sailed it to India.
    c. sailed it home to Great Britain.

6. Stanley found Livingstone
    a. on the upper Zambezi River.
    b. in the Kalahari Desert.
    c. near Lake Tanganyika.

7. Stanley was a
    a. reporter.
    b. doctor.
    c. missionary worker.

8. Before Livingstone discovered the Zambezi River, the rest of the world thought
    a. Africa had many rivers like the Nile.
    b. no one lived anywhere except on the coast.
    c. Africa was a large desert.

Name _____

DAVID LIVINGSTONE

OUT OF AFRICA

Use other books to help you find the correct answer in this matching exercise.

1. _____ diamonds
2. _____ polyrhythmic
3. _____ polygamy
4. _____ Nile River
5. _____ Dr. Albert Schweitzer
6. _____ African Nationalism
7. _____ savanna
8. _____ addax
9. _____ Watusi
10. _____ Livingstone
11. _____ veldt
12. _____ oasis
13. _____ okapi
14. _____ Pygmies
15. _____ deserts

a. cover two-fifths of Africa
b. these stones come from Africa.
c. different instruments played in different beats at the same time
d. builder of a hospital whose first operating room was a shed.
e. the feeling that Europeans should give up their power
f. part giraffe, part antelope, and part zebra
g. fertile place in the desert
h. when people have more than one spouse
i. kind of antelope that lives in Sahara
j. longest river in the world
k. people less than five feet tall
l. people seven to eight feet tall
m. grasslands in southern Africa; high plateau
n. warm and dry; one rainy month per year; treeless plain or flat open region
o. English missionary who explored Africa

Name _____

── DAVID LIVINGSTONE ──
AFRICAN SAFARI

Using encyclopedias and other books for reference, fill in the blank in front of each sentence with true or false. If you believe the statement to be false, write a corrected version of the sentence in the space above it.

____ 1. The Sahara Desert is the largest dry area of land in the world.

____ 2. The southern tip of Africa is called Cape Horn.

____ 3. The Nile river flows north into the Red Sea.

____ 4. The Zambezi River flows mainly into the Indian Ocean and the Mozambique Channel.

____ 5. Mt. Kenya is Africa's highest peak.

____ 6. Africa is smaller than the United States.

____ 7. Africa's chief rivers are the Congo, Limpopo, Niger, Nile, Orange, and Zambezi.

____ 8. The major deserts are the Kalahari, Sahara, and the Namib.

____ 9. Antananarivo is the capital of Libya.

____10. Somalia's capital is Addis Ababa.

— DAVID LIVINGSTONE —

THE DARK CONTINENT

Locate the following on the map. Label with the corresponding number.

1. Fourth largest island in the world
2. Longest river in the world
3. Largest desert in Africa
4. Capital of Ethiopia
5. Largest city in Africa
6. Fourth longest river in Africa; explored by Livingstone.
7. Third largest lake in the world
8. Highest peak in Africa

Neil
Armstrong

Neil Armstrong is one of the most famous of all the astronauts and cosmonauts. Born in Ohio in 1930, he received his pilot's license at age 16. Armstrong joined the navy and flew 78 combat missions during the Korean War. After he received a degree in aeronautical engineering from Purdue University, he became a test pilot for the National Aeronautics and Space Administration (NASA). In 1966 he made his first flight into space on *Gemini 8*.

During this flight *Gemini 8* had a malfunction which caused the spacecraft to tumble through space. However, Armstrong kept calm and regained control of the craft. His knowledge and his cool-headed reactions in dangerous situations are perhaps the reasons why he was chosen to lead the *Apollo 11* expedition to the moon.

The space age began before Armstrong made his first journey on *Gemini 8*. On October 4, 1957, the Russians launched *Sputnik* to orbit the earth. In November *Sputnik II* carried a dog named Laika, the first animal to travel in space. The United States entered the race in January 1958, with the *Explorer I. Vanguard I* followed in March. These two satellites were smaller and less powerful than the *Sputniks*.

On April 12, 1961, Yuri Gagarin, a Soviet cosmonaut, made an orbit around the earth. Alan Shepard, Jr., an American astronaut, rocketed into space on May 5, 1961.

In President John F. Kennedy's May 1961 Congressional address, he challenged the American people:

> Now it is time to take longer strides . . . time for this nation to take a clearly leading role in space achievement which in many ways may hold a clearly leading role in space achievement which in many ways may hold the key to our future on earth . . . I believe this nation should commit itself to achieving the goal . . . of landing a man on the moon and returning him safely to earth . . . .

The first American astronaut to orbit the earth was John Glenn. He traveled into space on February 20, 1962.

Eight years later on July 16, 1969, Edwin "Buzz" Aldrin, Neil Armstrong, and Michael Collins were launched in the *Apollo 11* spacecraft in an expedition to the moon.

The spacecraft had three parts: the Columbia, a command module; the Eagle, a lunar module; and a service module. The spacecraft was attached to a rocket called *Saturn*. The rocket and spacecraft were as tall as a 35 story building.

During liftoff, the earth shook up to 10 miles away. Mike Collins said of the spacecraft, "noise, yes, lots of it, but mostly motion, as we are thrown left and right against our straps in spasmodic little jerks."

Saturn had three engines and fuel tanks called stages. The first of Saturn's stages burned up its fuel and dropped off into the Atlantic Ocean. Three minutes after that, the second stage left the spacecraft. After orbiting the earth once, the astronauts fired the third rocket to go to the moon.

Apollo 11 orbited the earth 18,000 miles per hour. Collins separated the Columbia from the Saturn rocket which carried the Eagle, the lunar module, and Armstrong radioed to the Houston Space Center, "The Eagle has wings." Armstrong and Aldrin were on the Eagle. Collins stayed on the Columbia.

The astronauts entered cislunar space. This is the void between the earth and the moon that is black with streaks of sunlight. As they traveled for more than two days in this space, they kept busy monitoring the craft and talking with mission control.

The astronauts passed into equigravisphere, where the earth's gravitational force gives way to the moon's force. The Columbia slowed down as the moon pulled the spacecraft to its surface.

The moon's surface was covered with large boulders. To navigate around them, the astronauts had to use extra fuel. Armstrong very carefully avoided a near disaster by guiding the capsule onto a level area.

Back on earth, millions of people watching their televisions saw the landing but never knew how dangerous the event had been. On Sunday, July 20, Armstrong said, "The Eagle has landed."

When he stepped down the ladder onto the moon, he said the famous statement that would go down in history, "That's one small step for man, one giant leap for mankind." Nineteen minutes later, Aldrin joined him.

The moon's surface was fine and powdery. The sky around them was dark and the land was gray. The astronauts moved by hopping. Although each spacesuit weighed 500 pounds on earth, the lack of gravity made them weigh less than 100 pounds on the moon.

Armstrong and Aldrin placed a plaque on the moon that said, "Here men from planet Earth first set foot on the moon, July 1969, A.D. We came in peace for all mankind."

They left a shoulder patch of the *Apollo I* crew, who died in a spacecraft fire in 1967. The astronauts also left medals in memory of two Soviet cosmonauts who had died during a mission.

After they planted an American flag and saluted it, they talked to President Nixon on the phone. He said, "For one priceless moment in the whole history of man, all the people of this earth are truly one. One in their pride in what you have done, and one in our prayers that you return safely to earth."

The astronauts recorded temperatures of 234° Fahrenheit in the sun and -279° in the shade. They set up a seismometer to measure "moonquakes" and collected 50 pounds of rocks to take home. Three hours after the astronauts stepped onto the moon, they returned to the Eagle.

Everyone on earth waited anxiously. What if there were engine trouble? When the oxygen supplies ran out, the astronauts would die.

Fortunately, liftoff was successful and the Eagle docked with the Columbia. Later, they separated the Eagle again, and the Columbia returned to earth alone.

On July 24 the spacecraft entered the earth's atmosphere at 25,000 miles per hour. At a lower altitude and a slower speed, three parachutes were released and the capsule splashed down into the Pacific Ocean. Thirty minutes later, with flotation devices around the capsule, the hatch opened.

A diver gave the astronauts isolation suits. Armstrong, Aldrin, and Collins were sprayed with disinfectant as a precaution against any moon germs. A helicopter picked them up and landed the USS *Hornet*, a Navy ship. Although the astronauts spent nearly three weeks in a mobile quarantine trailer to prevent possible infection from spreading, no bacteria from the moon was ever discovered.

On the evening of July 20, someone placed a bouquet of flowers on President Kennedy's grave. A note attached to the flowers read, "Mr. President, the Eagle has landed."

► *Suggested Teaching Strategies*

For further research, students can read *Apollo and the Moon Landing* by Gregory Vogt (Millbrook Press) and *Apollo to the Moon* by Gregory P. Kennedy (Chelsea House); for astronomy projects they can read *Look to the Night Sky* by Seymour Simon (Puffin) and *Space and Astronomy* by Robert L. Bonnet and G. David Keen (TAB).

1. Have students draw the phases of the moon: a new moon, waxing crescent, first quarter, waxing gibbous (JIB-us), full, waning gibbous, third quarter, and waning crescent.

2. Students may make mobiles of the planets.

3. Students may compile information and sketches for one planet. Then have them present the information to the class.

4. Play "20 Questions" with students using the planet information that they have learned.

5. Students may research the spacesuit and draw and label its design.

6. Students may choose one of the following astronauts or astronomers to study:

   a. Valentina Tereshkova

   b. Sir Isaac Newton

   c. Johannes Kepler

   d. Robert Goddard

7. Have the class sketch diagrams of the *Apollo* spacecraft, complete with cabin capsule, rocket engine, and lunar lander.

8. President Kennedy said, ". . . space achievement . . . may hold the key to earth . . ." What did he mean by that statement? How can knowledge of space help us on earth? Have a class discussion and have students write essays on this topic.

9. Visit a planetarium. Students can find out how astronomers locate objects in the sky.

10. The class can make a time line of space exploration.

Name _____

JOURNEY TO THE MOON

After reading the article about Neil Armstrong, circle the correct answer.

1. The first person to orbit the earth was
   a. Alan Shepard, Jr.
   b. John Glenn.
   c. Yuri Gagarin.

2. The first satellite in space was
   a. *Sputnik.*
   b. *Vanguard.*
   c. *Explorer.*

3. *Apollo II* landed on the moon
   a. July 20, 1969.
   b. July 16, 1969.
   c. February 20, 1962.

4. The spacecraft that orbited, but did not land on the the moon, was called
   a. *Saturn.*
   b. *The Eagle.*
   c. *Columbia.*

5. How many people witnessed the event?
   a. 17 scientists from NASA
   b. 50,000
   c. millions

6. The temperature on the moon was recorded at
   a. 303° Fahrenheit.
   b. 234° Fahrenheit.
   c. 101° Fahrenheit.

7. The astronauts' spacesuits weighed
   a. less than 100 pounds on the moon.
   b. more than 200 pounds on the moon.
   c. about 50 pounds on the moon.

8. When the astronauts returned home, they landed
   a. in the Atlantic Ocean.
   b. in the Mohave Desert.
   c. in the Pacific Ocean.

Name _____

SPACE FACTS

Using encyclopedias and other books for reference, fill in the blanks with true or false. If you believe the statement to be false, write a corrected version of the sentence in the space above it.

_____1. It takes the Moon a month to travel around the Earth.

_____2. Twelve men have been to the moon between 1969 and 1972.

_____3. The spacecraft *Saturn* was attached to the rocket *Apollo*.

_____4. The first two rocket stages fell into the Pacific Ocean.

_____5. It takes the Earth a whole year to go around the Sun.

_____6. Gravity on the Moon is about one sixth of the gravity on Earth.

_____7. Neptune is nicknamed the Red Planet because its sand is made of red iron oxide.

_____8. Mars is located closer to Earth than any other planet.

_____9. The Moon is a satellite of Earth.

_____10. The Andromeda is the core of the Moon.

NEIL ARMSTRONG

SPACE TO LEARN

Write a paragraph answering each of the following questions. Use your library to research the answers.

1. What is the big bang theory?

   _____
   _____
   _____

2. What is a sunspot?

   _____
   _____
   _____

3. Explain zero gravity.

   _____
   _____
   _____

4. What is the theory of relativity?

   _____
   _____
   _____

5. Debate the statement, "More funds should go toward space travel." Do you agree or disagree? Why?

   _____
   _____
   _____

Name _____

NEIL ARMSTRONG

BLASTOFF! TO THE MOON

Across

2. The man who stayed with the spacecraft
3. The moment a rocket leaves the ground
4. An instrument used to see objects in space
5. Scientist who developed the theory of relativity
8. This form of oxygen absorbs the sun's ultraviolet rays.
10. A point in the sky above an observer
12. The most distant planet from the sun
13. Every material thing that exists is in this
14. A unit of measure in space—equal to 3.26 light years
16. An astronomer who has a comet named after him
18. The inner atmosphere of the sun

Down

1. This president spoke to the astronauts on the moon.
3. A constellation nicknamed "Little Bear"
6. A ball of gas that gives off energy through fusion
7. A star that explodes and shines brighter for awhile
9. In space, the path of an object moving around another object
11. The moment the spacecraft contacts the surface of Earth after a flight
15. Earth spins on this once every 24 hours.
17. When one body in space shadows or covers another body

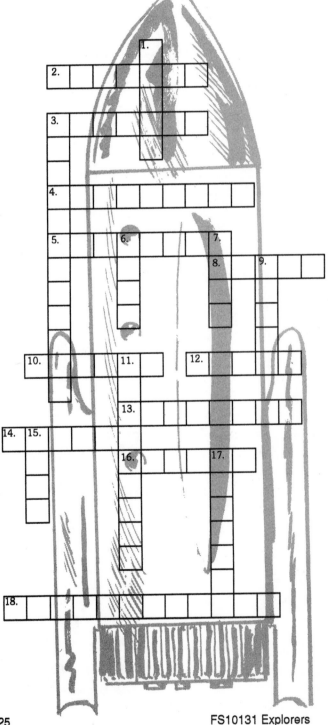

Name _____

— NEIL ARMSTRONG —

MOON COCOON

You are an astronaut on the moon.

1. What do you see on the moon? What is the atmosphere or mood?

   _____
   _____
   _____
   _____

2. Describe the moon's surface.

   _____
   _____
   _____
   _____

3. How does it feel to move around without gravity? What is it like to wear a pressure suit? (It is also called a moon cocoon!)

   _____
   _____
   _____
   _____

4. Astronaut Ellen Ochoa has said, "When you're in space, water stays in a ball in air. Then you can put straws in the ball and sip." Describe life in a space capsule. How do you eat? Sleep? (An interesting fact: The astronaut's bathroom has a toilet with straps to hold the user down!)

   _____
   _____
   _____
   _____

Captain
Cook

Born in England in 1728, James Cook worked on his family farm until he was 17 when he moved to a fishing port. James got a job in a store, but he really wanted a life at sea so he was apprenticed to a coal shipper for 10 years. He lived with the ship owner, John Walker, who taught him the science of navigation. James was so interested in it, he read everything he could to learn more.

Although Walker offered him a job to command one of his ships, Cook decided to join the Royal Navy. In 1758, after a few years as a volunteer seaman, Cook became a master to the captain. As master, he was in charge of navigating and sailing the ship.

During the Seven Years War (1756-1763) he surveyed the St. Lawrence River for the navy. Because of the information that he supplied, Great Britain captured the French city of Quebec, Canada. One hundred years later, navigators were still using his charts. In 1768 the navy sent Cook on the ship, *Endeavor,* to take astronomers to Tahiti to study a rare (or uncommon) occurrence. Scientists of the Royal Society in London wanted to witness the passing of Venus between the Earth and the Sun, and with Cook's help, were able to study the event. It was important that they witness the Transit of Venus in many different places to compare their results because the Transit would not occur again until 1874–nearly 100 years later.

The British Government was interested in Cook's expedition for another reason. They knew there was a continent in the South Pacific, and they thought it kept the world in balance. They called it *Terra Australis.* Great Britain hoped Cook would find it.

In ship voyages, scurvy was a common and often deadly disease that plagued sailors. Symptoms included bleeding gums, loss of teeth and appetite, and blood infections which could cause death. Sailors got the disease because they did not have fresh fruits and vegetables on their long journeys. Their diet consisted mostly of salt beef and dry biscuits. But Cook made certain his crew had concentrated lemon juice and sauerkraut so no outbreak of the disease occurred. He took other precautions as well. Bedding was aired on the deck, and the lower rooms of the ship were ventilated.

The most dangerous part of the trip was traveling around South American's Cape Horn. The Horn was known for terrible storms that wrecked ships. But Cook knew the worst weather occurred after March, so he sailed around the Horn in January.

In April 1769, Cook reached Tahiti. He had gone farther south than anyone had ever gone before. While there, he became friendly with the Tahitian chiefs, Tupia and Tutaha. Cook's crew built a fort at Point Venus to set up scientific equipment to observe the Transit of Venus. Astronomer Charles Green, botanist Daniel Carl Solander, and Cook observed the event. "We very distinctly saw an atmosphere or dusky shade around the body of the planet," wrote Cook.

Cook left Tahiti in July 1769. Tupia joined the crew as a helpful guide and interpreter when they visited the islands west of Tahiti. Since the explorers did not sight Terra Australis, they headed north and reached New Zealand. There they met the Maori warriors who did not appreciate strangers invading their territory. After many attempts to send men ashore, under Maoris attacks, Cook's crew had to fire in self-defense. Several Maoris were killed, and Cook was always ashamed that this had happened. Unlike many other explorers during that time, Cook did not feel that island natives were inferior to the British.

For six months, Cook traveled around New Zealand. He discovered that it was actually two islands, and not an extension of a southern continent, which people believed before his journey. He was the first explorer to create a map of New Zealand.

In March of 1770, the *Endeavor* sailed west and found the east coast of Australia. Cook mapped Botany Bay and Sydney Harbor. He named it Botany because of the many new plants that the botanist and naturalist collected there.

In June the ship entered the Great Barrier Reef, an area (of over 1,200 miles long) that is dangerous for ships. Although the sharp, jagged corals were beautiful, they made navigation difficult. The ship traveled slowly, but it crashed on June 11.

Cook wrote, "The hole was cut away as if it had been done by the hand of man with a blunt edge tool."

To make it to shore, the crew stretched a sail over the hole. They stayed a few weeks to make repairs. (The area is now called Cooktown.) The crew camped ashore and searched for fruit and green plants to eat; they hunted turtles and kangaroos for meat.

After a few weeks, they headed home. Cook followed the coast north, stopped in the East Indies, and traveled across the Indian and Atlantic Oceans. In July 1771, he and his crew arrived in England, nearly three years after the journey had begun.

Cook received a hero's welcome and King George III named him commander. A year later he embarked on a journey which began Antarctic exploration. Because of his near fatal experience in the Barrier Reef, Cook took two ships, the *Resolution* and the *Adventure*. He used the first chronometer, a ship's clock which timed the voyage and helped the men calculate their east-west longitude.

The *Resolution* and the *Adventure* crossed the Antarctic Circle in January 1773. The crew had to deal with extreme cold, uncontrollable winds, fog, and huge mountains of ice. Crew members lowered smaller boats to break off samples from the ice, and they discovered the ice provided fresh water. Although Cook sailed around the Antarctic and came within 75 miles of the mainland, they were not able to see the "last continent" because of the icebergs.

On Cook's third and last journey, he searched for a "Northwest Passage" to link the Atlantic and Pacific Oceans. They left Plymouth, Massachusetts, in July 1776 for New Zealand and Tahiti. From there Cook planned to cross the Pacific and land at "New Alboon" (near what is now San Francisco). He discovered Christmas Island on December 24 and reached the Hawaiian Islands in 1778. He was the first European to visit them.

The Hawaiians bowed before him and thought he was their god, "Lono." Cook stayed two weeks and in February, he left for America. In April he and his crew stopped at Nootka Sound, Canada, to repair broken masts and then continued sailing along the coast of British Columbia, Alaska, and the Aleutian Islands.

In August the ships began sailing through the Bering Strait but soon came upon ice that barred their passage. They turned back to rest on the Hawaiian Islands. The natives gave the crew food but did not understand why the gods gave no gifts in return. They especially wanted things made of iron, so they swam out to the ships and dug nails out of the vessels' sides with chisels!

The ships left in February but ran into bad weather which damaged the *Resolution's* foremast. Upon returning to Hawaii to make repairs, they found the Hawaiians unhappy to see them. The natives had discovered the men were not gods but only humans, since one sailor had died of a stroke. Since the Hawaiians had fed the crew before, their supplies were low and they were not looking forward to sharing any more food with them.

Natives began to steal things, and when the ship's much needed cutter (large boat with oars) was stolen, Cook knew they had to do something to get it back. He tried to trick a chief into boarding the ship to keep him until the cutter was returned. However, the Hawaiians attacked and Cook was killed. His body was buried at sea by his crew.

Cook's journeys allowed naturalists on his ships to record 3,600 plant species and over 1,000 types of animals. In 11 years Cook had explored Eastern Australia, New Zealand, many South Pacific islands, the Hawaiian Islands, and the Alaskan coast. He is said to be the first explorer of the Antarctic Circle.

▶ *Suggested Teaching Strategies*

Students can further research Captain Cook's journeys. Some sources are *Captain Cook* by Alan Blackwood (Bookwright Press), *The Voyages of Captain Cook* by Jason Hook (Bookwright Press), and *The Voyages of Captain Cook* by Dorothy and Thomas Hoobler (Putnam).

1. Have students sketch a ship like those on which Cook traveled. Label parts such as the tiller, mizzenmast, wheel, hold, pumps, mainmast, cutter, foremast, anchor, and bowsprit.

2. The class may create posters about Australian animals. Include drawings of the animal, its habitat, and the food it eats. Some of Australia's famous native animals include koalas, wallabies, wombats, and kangaroos.

3. Today Tahiti is considered a tropical paradise. Students may role play they are travel agents and plan a trip to this island. They must keep a financial record of the costs and a calendar of the places they will visit.

4. After reading about Tahiti, students can write journals about their trips.

5. Using photographs of the Great Barrier Reef, students may use colored pencils to sketch these beautiful corals.

6. Students may produce a show like *Sixty Minutes* all about explorers. The class chooses four explorers to study and "interview" on camera. If possible, videotape the show so that the class can view it afterwards.

7. Have the class create a newspaper dated 1771, when Cook returned to England. They may research England's history to write a variety of articles for the paper.

8. Students may make a world map with a key to label Cook's journeys. Have them use colored markers to show the different trips.

9. Students may write an essay about what an *atoll* is. They can use Christmas Island (also called Kiritimati Atoll) as an example.

10. The class may decorate a bulletin board using Captain Cook's adventures. Let them try to tell a story without using words.

Name _____

CAPTAIN COOK

COOK'S STEW

After reading about Captain Cook, circle the correct answer.

1. James Cook sailed on the _____ to Tahiti to witness an important event in astronomy.
   a. *Adventure*
   b. *Resolution*
   c. *Endeavor*

2. This event was
   a. the passage of Venus between the Earth and the Sun.
   b. the solar eclipse.
   c. the passage of Venus between the Earth and the Moon.

3. Cook's ship was damaged while traveling through the Great Barrier Reef. The crew
   a. plugged the hole using large timber planks and canvas sacks.
   b. stretched a sail over the hole.
   c. towed the ship ashore with a cutter.

4. Cook learned a lesson from his first trip. On his second journey he
   a. brought fruits and vegetables so the men would not get sick as they had when they sailed the first time.
   b. took two ships.
   c. took gifts for the natives.

5. The natives of Hawaii wanted
   a. objects made of iron.
   b. jewels for ornaments.
   c. a chronometer since they thought it had magical powers.

6. On Cook's third journey, bad weather at this location forced the crew to turn back to Hawaii.
   a. Bering Strait
   b. Antarctic Circle
   c. Cape Horn

7. Cook was the first explorer of
   a. the Bering Strait.
   b. the Antarctic Circle.
   c. Cape Horn.

8. On Cook's last trip, he discovered
   a. Australia.
   b. New Zealand.
   c. Christmas Island.

CAPTAIN COOK

EXPLORING

Using other books to help you, write a paragraph on each of the following topics.

1. What was the Seven Years War?

   _____

   _____

   _____

   _____

2. Describe the life styles of the original Maoris.

   _____

   _____

   _____

   _____

3. Define the word *transit* as it is used in astronomy.

   _____

   _____

   _____

   _____

4. Cook's journeys took place between 1768 and 1779. List some of the events that happened in America during this time period.

   _____

   _____

   _____

   _____

Name _____

CAPTAIN COOK

SOUTH SEAS

Using encyclopedias and other books for reference, fill in the blank in front of each sentence with true or false. If you believe the statement to be false, write a corrected version of the sentence in the space above it.

_____ 1. The largest of the Hawaiian main islands are Kauai, Oahu, Maui, and Hawaii.

_____ 2. Honolulu, the state capital, is located on the island of Hawaii.

_____ 3. The Bering Strait is located at 66 1/2° N and 170° W.

_____ 4. A small island off the southern coast of Australia is called Sri Lanka.

_____ 5. Hawaii's highest elevation is Mt. Kauna.

_____ 6. New Zealand is about 1,000 miles southeast of Australia.

_____ 7. New Zealand consists of three islands.

_____ 8. The capital of New Zealand is Wellington, located on the North Island.

_____ 9. Christmas Island lies about 1,300 miles south of Honolulu.

_____10. Cape Horn is on the southern tip of South America.

Name _____

CAPTAIN COOK

SOUTH PACIFIC

Using the clues below, fill in the correct answers in the crossword grid.

Across

2. Barrier _____
5. Distance measured in degrees north or south of the equator
7. Distance measured in degrees east or west of a line running north and south through Greenwich, England
11. Half of the globe
12. This clock times a voyage to help place the ship's longitude.
13. A coral island shaped like a ring
14. State separated from Asia by the Bering Strait

Down

1. A ship's smaller boat driven by oars
2. This is attached to the rear of the ship and is used for steering.
3. Scientist who studies plants
4. The science of directing the course of a ship
6. A disease caused by poor nutrition
8. Imaginary circle around the middle of the earth, midway between the North and South Poles
9. A state that is a group of islands
10. Person learning a trade
12. Captain _____

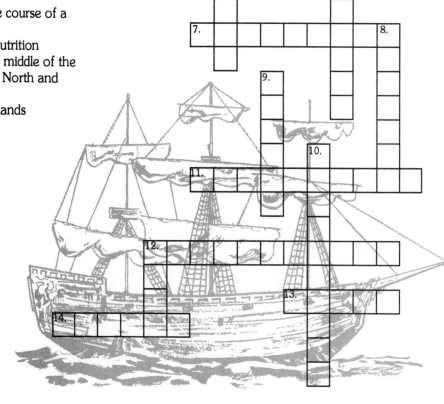

Admiral **Peary**

Born in Pennsylvania on May 6, 1856, Robert Peary grew up fascinated with explorer Elisha Kent Kane's 1853-1856 adventures in the Arctic. Since the 1500s, many people had tried to reach the North Pole but failed because of the ice and bad weather. Sailors died while trying to find a Northwest Passage from the Atlantic Ocean to the Pacific Ocean.

As an adult, Peary became a civil engineer and joined the United States Navy. While in the navy, he traveled through Nicaragua to find canal routes between the two major oceans. As he explored hot and humid jungles, he longed to lead an expedition to the Arctic.

Peary requested many temporary leaves from the navy so he could fulfill his dream. He traveled to Greenland in 1886 and again in 1891. Peary went farther into Greenland's interior than anyone had ever gone before. On his second trip there, Dr. Frederick Cook, a surgeon, and Matthew Henson, Peary's assistant, joined his expedition. Peary's wife came along and gave birth to their daughter, Marie. Eskimos called the child "Snow Baby."

He journeyed to the Arctic five more times within the next 15 years mapping uncharted areas. On one of those trips, he had to have eight toes amputated by the crew's doctor, Thomas Dedrick. (His toes had been frozen and the infection would have endangered his life had they not been removed.) After recuperating six weeks at a camp on Grant Land, he taught himself how to walk again.

While on the expedition of 1893-1895, Peary took three meteorites from Greenland and sold them to a museum for $40,000. He needed the money to fund his explorations. Peary did not seem to care that he had taken the Eskimo's only source of metal.

Unfortunately, although he was a great explorer, Robert Peary was not known for his humanitarian acts. He did not respect the Eskimos. "Of what use are Eskimos to the world?" he wrote. "They are too far removed to be of any value for commercial enterprises. . . ."

While in Greenland, he robbed several Eskimo graves. Two Eskimos on his crew, Nooktah and Kessuh, died from illness during an expedition. Instead of returning the remains to their families for proper burial, Peary took them back to America to sell them to a museum. His actions reportedly caused one Eskimo to say Americans were "a race of scientific criminals."

In 1908 Peary led an expedition on his ship, the *Roosevelt*. His crew included the ship's captain, a dog team driver, an igloo builder, and an engineering professor. His assistant, Henson, accompanied Peary on all of his trips. Since Henson spoke the Eskimo language, he served as an interpreter for Peary.

Before they left, President Roosevelt boarded the ship and wished them luck. On July 6, 1908, the crew sailed for Greenland. Within a few weeks, they reached Etah on Greenland's Coast. For the expedition, Peary hired 17 Eskimos and bought dozens of dogs to pull sledges.

The next few weeks the ship slowly edged its way through the ice. "The constant jolting, bumping, and jarring against the ice packs . . The sudden stops and starts and the frequent storms made work and comfort aboard the ship all but impossible," said Henson.

At Cape Sheridan they left the *Roosevelt* for travel on land. The dogs moved their supplies on sledges through the snow and ice to Cape Columbia, 90 miles away. The sledges often weighed over 700 pounds! Instead of camping in tents, they built strong igloos to keep them warm and in which to store supplies. Peary and his men wore furs and they ate dried meat (or musk oxen and deer when they could hunt), biscuits, condensed milk, and tea.

Peary divided his crew into teams. The first team would create a trail using axes to cut away ice. It was slow and difficult. One man said, "You had to fight for every yard gain, as you'd do on the football field."

The men made camps where they would leave supplies. Then the first team would return to Cape Columbia to rest. Peary was on the last team, for he hoped to be able to travel 130 miles to the Pole. They left Cape Columbia on February 18, 1909.

Three sledges broke through the ice causing damage that required repair. They worked bare handed in -50° temperatures. Peary and his men battled fierce snowstorms, shifting ice, and big snow drifts. The men sank knee-deep in snow.

They came upon a gap in the ice a quarter mile wide. Water stretched between the ice crack. Unable to cross, they tried to sleep. However, during the night, the ice moved with a terrifying shaking and grinding and the men were able to move northward.

36

The next break in the ice, "The Big Lead," took a week to cross. While waiting, the crew boxed, wrestled, and raced. Finally, new ice formed over the gap.

During the expedition, supplies ran low, and the men were forced to kill some of the dogs for food. Exhaustion, danger, and hunger forced some of the men to turn back. But Peary pushed on with 5 sledges, 40 dogs, and 5 men. On April 6, 1909, he made camp and planted a flag into the snow on top of his igloo. He figured they had reached the 89° parallel.

Peary wrote in his journal, "The Pole at last!!! . . . my dream and ambition for 23 years. Mine at last." He left two notes and a strip of his polar flag in a glass jar at the camp. Peary, Henson, and the Eskimos that had come with him held flags and posed for a photograph.

The return trip to Cape Columbia took only 17 days. The group rested and then boarded the *Roosevelt*.

However, controversy arose when Dr. Frederick Cook (the surgeon that joined Peary on his second trip to Greenland), claimed that *he* had reached the North Pole earlier. Data from both men were examined by experts. The National Geographic Society supported Peary, but some people would not accept his claim. Congress investigated and gave Peary the credit.

Peary wrote *Nearest the Pole* and *The North Pole* about his experiences. Admiral Robert Peary died on February 20, 1920, of a blood disease. He was 63. The flag he had carried on his expeditions was placed on his coffin.

▶ *Suggested Teaching Strategies*

Students can read more about Admiral Peary. Some sources are *Peary to the Pole* by Walter Lord (Harper and Row), *The Story of Admiral Peary at the North Pole* by Zachary Kent (Children's Press), and *Robert Peary and the Quest for the North Pole* by Christopher Dwyer (Chelsea House).

1. After reading about sledges and igloos, students may make sketches and create models of them.

2. Ask students what Peary's polar flag looked like. Have them recreate it out of cloth. Next, students can participate in a discussion on flags and symbols. Students will design a flag to represent their school, classroom, family, or themselves.

3. Students may write a short story about survival. It does not have to take place in the Arctic.

4. Using crushed ice, students can create a frozen treat! Have them write down the directions to their recipe in clear and concise language.

5. Have students "take sides" and write an opinion essay on the Arctic controversy of Peary vs. Cook.

6. Robert Peary's birthday is May 6. The class can come up with fun ways to celebrate it using the theme of the North Pole.

7. Each student will read a book about the Arctic and write a book review. Using these book reviews, the class can create its own guidelines on what makes a good book and what elements are necessary in writing nonfiction.

8. How have explorers exploited natives throughout history? Students may discuss this topic using specific examples.

9. Students will make a weather map of the United States and predict the weather, using symbols. Students should include a key. Beneath the map, they can write a paragraph describing their predictions.

10. Divide students into groups to report on one of the following: blizzards, lightning, tornadoes, fog, or hurricanes. Students may use charts, diagrams, pictures, and experiments in their reports.

Name _____

THE LAND OF ICE

After reading about Admiral Peary, circle the correct answer.

1. Peary admired this explorer who visited the Arctic during the years 1853-1856.
   a. Richard Byrd
   b. Elisha Kent Kane
   c. Henry Hudson

2. While in the navy, Peary explored
   a. Nicaragua.
   b. Argentina.
   c. Ethiopia.

3. On his expeditions, Peary
   a. admired the Eskimos for their survival skills.
   b. thought the Eskimos were superior to Americans.
   c. wanted to use the Eskimos for his own gain.

4. "The Big Lead" was
   a. the first dog sledge team to arrive at the North Pole.
   b. a large gap in the ice.
   c. the race between explorers to the Arctic.

5. Peary reached his destination in
   a. 1881.
   b. 1919.
   c. 1909.

6. Peary sailed in his ship, the_____.
   a. *McKinley*
   b. *Wilson*
   c. *Roosevelt*

7. This man claimed that he reached the North Pole before Peary.
   a. Frederick Cook
   b. Henry Hanson
   c. Thomas Dedrick

8. Peary left Cape Columbia on February 18. He reached the North Pole on
   a. March 17.
   b. April 6.
   c. June 1.

WEATHER STATION

On expeditions, explorers keep track of the weather conditions. You can do this, too, by creating a weather station.

1. Get an inexpensive thermometer to measure temperature.

2. Make a rain gauge to measure precipitation. Cut the top off a clear plastic bottle. Fit the top upside down into the remainder of the bottle to form a funnel. With a ruler, mark the scale on the side of the bottle. Place your rain gauge in an open place and put it firmly in the ground.

3. Make a wind vane out of balsa wood to show the direction of the wind. (A wind vane looks like an arrow.) Insert a pin through a bead and then through the center of the shaft of the vane. Put another bead on the pin; then stick the pin into the top of a wooden dowel. Check to see that it spins freely. A compass will show you where north and south are located.

4. Measure wind speed with a wind gauge or anemometer. Glue a Ping Pong ball onto a piece of thread and tie it to the center of a protractor. Hold the protractor parallel to the wind to read the angle of the ball. (Ninety degrees equals 0 miles per hour, and each degree is approximately 1 mile per hour.)

5. If you have snow, use a yardstick to measure the depth. Compute the average of several measurements to record the snowfall. Do not measure drifted snow.

6. Record all of the readings of your weather instruments noting the date and time in a notebook.

7. With colored pencils, sketch the clouds in the sky. Go to the library and find a book about weather to serve as a resource to help you label the types of clouds that you have drawn.

ICE

The Eskimos knew how to use their environment to survive the extreme cold in the Arctic. Peary learned from them. Igloo shelters were made by cutting blocks of frozen snow. Although the walls began to melt when stoves inside were lit, the Eskimos would open a door to make the water freeze into ice. This stopped heat from escaping.

When water freezes and it becomes ice, it expands. Ice is lighter than water, so it floats. Ice takes up only one-ninth more space than water, so icebergs only show one-ninth of their form above water. Nine times that amount of ice is below the water's surface.

Conduct the following experiment to show that ice expands and takes up more space than water.

Fill a small plastic bottle with water. With aluminum foil, cover the top. Place the bottle in the freezer.

After the water has frozen, check the aluminum foil. The ice has pushed it above the rim of the bottle.

41

Name _____

─ADMIRAL PEARY─
WEATHER BUREAU

In 1870 Congress set up a national weather service as part of the United States Army. In 1891 the Weather Bureau was created under the Department of Agriculture. The Bureau provides data of weather, climate, daily forecasts, and warnings of dangerous weather conditions.

Meteorologists operate weather stations in our states, on islands in the Caribbean and the Pacific, from ships in the Atlantic, and from stations in the Arctic within eight degrees of the North Pole.

Read about weather to answer the following questions.

1. What is a physical meteorologist? _____
_____

2. A dynamic meteorologist? _____
_____

3. A synoptic meteorologist? _____
_____

4. What is a climatologist? _____
_____

5. Where can a weatherperson be employed? _____
_____

ADMIRAL PEARY

STEP BACK INTO HISTORY

This is a time line of events that occurred while Peary conducted his explorations. Write a report about one of these historical topics. Use index cards to organize your paper. Include footnotes and a bibliography of your resources.

1885 Canadian-Pacific Railroad completed.
1886 Haymarket Street Riots occur in Chicago.
1886 Statue of Liberty given by France to the United States.
1888 Eastman invents Kodak box camera.
1898 Spanish-American War begins.
1900 William McKinley is reelected president.
1900 Railroad engineer, Casey Jones, dies and becomes a folk hero.
1901 After McKinley's assassination, Theodore Roosevelt becomes president.
1902 Cuba receives independence.
1903 The Wright brothers make the first flight.
1904 Subway opens in New York.
1908 Model T Ford produced.
1909 William Taft is elected president.

Become a newspaper reporter and cover Peary's expeditions. Choose one of Peary's adventures on this time line and create a newspaper headline, article, cartoon, editorial, and letters to the editor about it.

1885 Travels to Nicaragua to survey what is later called the Panama Canal.
1886 Explores Greenland's interior.
1887 Leads the canal survey project in Panama.
1891-1895 Tries to sail up Smith Sound to reach the North Pole.
1905 Goes farthest north but does not get to the North Pole.
1908 Begins another expedition to the Pole.
1909 Reaches the North Pole.

Name _____

ADMIRAL PEARY

NORTH TO THE POLE

Identify the following places on the map. Label with the corresponding number. The black dot is the approximate location of the North Pole.

1. Beaufort Sea
2. Canada
3. Baffin Bay
4. Greenland
5. Victoria Island
6. Ellesmere Island
7. Baffin Island
8. Devon Island

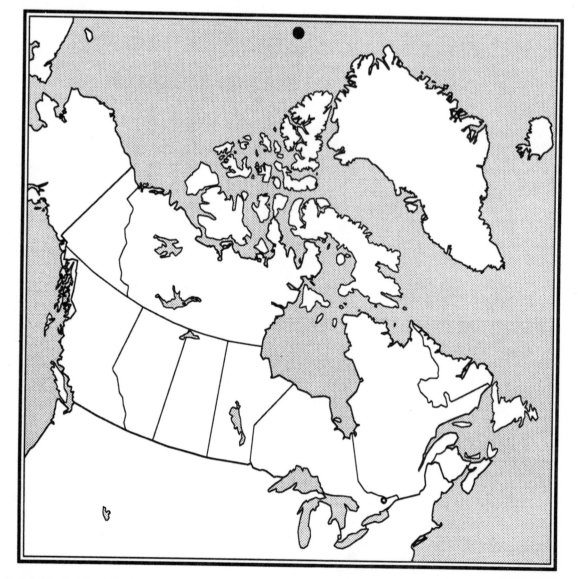

Ferdinand
Magellan

Ferdinand Magellan was born around the year 1480. As a child he was a page for King John of Portugal. At the court, his teacher taught him geography and navigation and told exciting stories about the explorers, Christopher Columbus and Vasco da Gama.

He longed to go to sea. But King John was murdered and his brother-in-law, Duke Manuel, became King. King Manuel did not have an interest in the sea and he did not like Magellan. But the new king did love riches.

In those days before refrigeration, spices preserved food. Arab traders brought spices from the East to Europe. King Manuel wanted the Portuguese traders to take over the spice trade. Therefore, in 1505 the king had Magellan sail to the east coast of Africa to battle Arab ships. But Magellan did not want to fight; he wanted to explore.

When he returned to Portugal, the king was pleased with his victory. As a reward, he made Magellan a commander of a ship to sail down the Malaca Strait to the Spice Islands. (The Spice Islands are now part of Indonesia.) On this expedition Magellan discovered the Philippine Islands.

Magellan learned that the Treaty of Tordesillas had been signed. In this agreement Portugal and Spain were to share the newly discovered lands. They divided the world with an imaginary line running north to south through Brazil. Spain took the new territory west of this line; Portugal owned the area east of the division. Magellan thought the Philippines were so far to the east they might belong to Spain. King Manuel was furious.

In 1513 Magellan was injured when he went on a military expedition to Morocco. The injury made him lame for the rest of his life. He came back to Portugal and asked for a ship to sail around the South American continent to search for a shorter route to the Far East and the Spice Islands. But King Manuel called him "club foot" and would not consent.

Magellan studied astronomy and navigation until he met Duarte Barbosa, a sea captain who lived in Spain. Although it was unusual for Spain and Portugal to work together, as they had always been rivals, King Charles I of Spain funded the voyage. As Magellan prepared for the expedition, he learned that King Manuel had sent spies to try to stop him.

On September 20, 1519, Magellan's five ships, the *San Antonio, Trinidad, Victoria, Concepcion,* and *Santiago* set sail. There were 241 men in his crew. Seven days later they reached Tenerife, one of the Canary Islands. But problems plagued the voyage.

Because of the competition between Spain and Portugal, the captains and Magellan had disagreements. One captain, Juan de Cartagena, tried to organize a rebellion. Magellan found out about it and put him in chains.

Turbulent storms caused what the sailors called "St. Elmo's Fire." The electricity in the air caused the ships to glow and flicker. The sailors thought St. Elmo, the patron saint of seamen, was protecting them. Near the equator the ships floated into the doldrums, where the sea was so calm there was no wind. For over three weeks, the ships lay on these waters. The hot sun melted the tar in the timbers causing leaks.

Finally, they drifted out of the doldrums. The winds helped direct them back on course. In December they reached Rio de Janeiro, Brazil. The crews repaired their ships, got fresh food and water, and made friends with the natives. On Christmas Day they departed southward.

Winter storms hit and the ships became coated with ice making them top-heavy. Magellan was worried they might capsize. Using an hourglass and compass, he led the ships down the coast of South America to the harbor of San Julian.

Three captains mutinied because they wanted to sail their ships, the *San Antonio, Victoria,* and *Concepcion*, home to Spain. But Magellan blocked the entrance of the harbor with his two ships, the *Trinidad* and *Santiago*. He recaptured the other three vessels, but one captain, Luis de Mendoza, was killed during the uprising. Another captain, Gasparde Quesada, was later given a trial and put to death. Other crew members were forced to work on the ships in chains.

Magellan and his men spent the winter at San Julian. They made log cabins for shelter. Antonio Pigafetta, a reporter for the expedition, chronicled their adventures in a journal.

They were the first white men to see "sea wolves with large teeth and no legs" (penguins and seals). The explorers met people that were over seven feet tall. They nicknamed the area "Land of the Big Feet."

Magellan and his men made friends with these large people, but Magellan made the mistake of trying to capture two of them to take back to Spain. After a fight in which a crew member was killed, Magellan set sail. He was afraid the giants might organize an attack against them.

They spent the rest of the winter in an inlet of the Santa Cruz River. The *Santiago* was destroyed by storm and all but one of the crew survived.

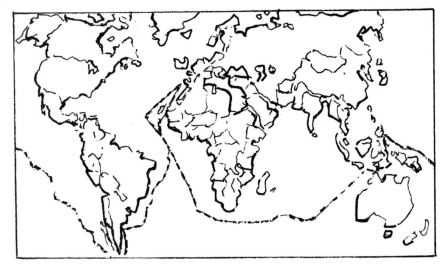

In October of 1520, the men finally discovered the passage to the Pacific—a deep and narrow strait now known as the Strait of Magellan. While Magellan was navigating through this passage, the captain and crew of the *San Antonio* went against Magellan's orders and headed back to Spain.

Magellan thought that within days they would reach the Spice Islands. But after weeks, he realized his calculations were wrong. They sailed into the tropics and ran out of food and water. The men were forced to eat rats, maggots, leather, and sawdust. The crew came down with scurvy, and 19 men died before they reached Guam on March 6, 1521.

They met waring natives who fought with the crew, so they stayed only long enough to get some fresh food and drink. Then they left for the Philippines where they found the Filipinos to be friendly and generous. The men ate fresh fruit, vegetables, and fish. They traded knives and mirrors for pearls, gold, and more food. Unfortunately, Magellan was not content to explore. He wanted to convert the natives to Christianity. He landed on the Mactan Island where he was attacked and killed.

The *Victoria* was the only ship to return to Spain. It was the first vessel to sail all the way around the world. According to Pigafetta's journals, their voyage covered 50,610 miles. In addition, Magellan had charted over 1,200 miles of South America's coast, had discovered and crossed the Pacific Ocean, and proved that the world was round.

► Suggested Teaching Strategies

Students can read more about Magellan. Some sources are *Ferdinand Magellan* by Alan Blackwood (Bookwright Press), *Ferdinand Magellan* by Sergio Bitossi (Silver Burdett), and *Magellan: First Around the World* by Ronald Syme (Morrow).

1. After reading about various spices, have students grow some of their own.

2. Students will make a map of their school or town. They should incorporate as many details as possible and include a key.

3. The Renaissance was the cultural movement during Magellan's time. Shakespeare, although born after Magellan's life, was a major force in literature during the Renaissance. Have the class read scenes from one of William Shakespeare's plays. Then view the play on film or as a performance on stage.

4. Students may create a model of the Globe Theatre.

5. Students may study the work of Leonardo Da Vinci, Michelangelo, Raphael, and Greco. They can choose one work of art to describe in an essay.

6. Leonardo da Vinci was also known for his creative inventions. His designs included an experimental flying machine, a movable bridge, and a construction crane. Many times inventions improve our lives, but sometimes they have negative consequences. What invention would the students like to "uninvent"? Have a class discussion on this topic.

7. Have a Renaissance Fair in your class or school! Students can make and wear costumes of the era, listen or play an opera or a fugue (composers during this time include Orlando di Lasso or Giovanni Palestrina), and display art work they have created. They may also perform scenes from one of Shakespeare's plays.

8. Using papier-mache or a ball, students make a globe marking Magellan's voyage of 1519-1522. (They can trace countries on paper and cut them out to serve as outlines.)

9. First there was the Penguin in the *Batman* series. Then came Opus in the cartoons. Have students create a quirky penguin character and use him or her in a humorous short story.

10. Students will plan their own expedition. Where are they going? How will they get there? They can write to travel bureaus for information. Where will they stay? Students should keep journals of their itineraries. They can read about their destination and pretend they are there. Each student then will write a letter to a friend describing his or her trip.

Name _____

PASSAGE TO THE PACIFIC

After reading about Ferdinand Magellan, circle the correct answer.

1. Ferdinand Magellan worked as a page for King John of
   a. Spain.
   b. Austria.
   c. Portugal.

2. The Treaty of Tordesillas declared
   a. Portugal and Spain would share land.
   b. Portugal and Spain would join forces in exploration.
   c. there would be peace between Portugal and Spain.

3. Magellan wanted to sail around South America to
   a. spread Christianity to South Americans.
   b. find a shorter route to the Far East.
   c. prove to King Manuel that the world was round.

4. St. Elmo's fire refers to
   a. a fire that was set on board by a captain during a mutiny.
   b. times when sailors had bonfires on land to honor their patron saint.
   c. electricity in the air from storms that caused strange light.

5. The term *doldrums at sea* means
   a. "an area of the ocean without wind."
   b. "the boredom sailors experienced while on a ship."
   c. "stormy, turbulent weather off a coastline."

6. Magellan and his crew were the first white men ever to see
   a. flying fish.
   b. penguins.
   c. an octopus.

7. While at San Julian, the explorers met
   a. giant people.
   b. Pygmies.
   c. cannibals.

8. Magellan finally discovered the passage to the Pacific in
   a. 1692.
   b. 1453.
   c. 1520.

49

Name _____

YOU ARE THERE

You are traveling with Magellan's expedition on one of his ships.

1. Who are you? What is your job on the ship?

   _____
   _____
   _____

2. Describe what you saw when you were in "St. Elmo's Fire."

   _____
   _____
   _____

3. Write about your experiences at San Julian. What did you feel when you saw the large men over seven feet tall? What about the new animals you have never seen before?

   _____
   _____
   _____

4. What happened during the mutiny? Which side did you choose?

   _____
   _____
   _____

FERDINAND MAGELLAN

WHO'S WHO

Use your library to discover what these people did. Match the letter to the correct number.

_____ 1. Bartolomeu Diaz

_____ 2. William Shakespeare

_____ 3. Raphael

_____ 4. Vasco da Gama

_____ 5. Michelangelo

_____ 6. Juan Ponce de Leon

_____ 7. Leonardo da Vinci

_____ 8. Desiderius Erasmus

_____ 9. Copernicus

_____ 10. Galileo

a. discovered Florida

b. known for painting the *Mona Lisa*

c. discovered the Cape of Good Hope

d. first person to use a telescope in astronomy

e. astronomer believed the earth and planets revolved around the sun

f. painted *School of Athens*

g. a priest and scholar, wrote *The Praise of Folly*

h. painted the ceiling of the Sistine Chapel

i. sailed to India

j. wrote *The Taming of the Shrew*

FERDINAND MAGELLAN

WHERE IN THE WORLD?

Where did these men explore? Go on your own expedition to find the answers.

Explorer	Place	Date
1. Bartolomeu Diaz		
2. Sir Richard Burton		
3. Louis Joliet		
4. Richard Byrd		
5. William R. Anderson		
6. William Clark		
7. Sieur de La Salle		
8. Pasha Emin		
9. Alexander the Great		
10. Leif Ericson		

FERDINAND MAGELLAN

SHIP AHOY!

Using the clues below, fill in the correct answers in the crossword grid.

Across

2. St. _____ Fire
3. Magellan was born in this country.
5. The Treaty of _____
7. Magellan was killed on this island.
9. When seamen rebel against their officers
10. This country funded Magellan's voyage to find a shorter route to the Pacific.
14. Magellan discovers these islands in 1512 and says they may belong to Spain.
17. Magellan put mutinous sailors in _____.
18. Antonio _____served as a reporter for Magellan's voyage.

Down

1. The period from 1400-1600
4. A part of the ocean where there is very little wind
6. The _____of Magellan
8. Magellan was injured in battle. This injury caused him to _____.
11. Magellan and his crew were the first white men to see these animals.
12. People were interested in the _____trade and also the _____Islands.
13. This ship was the first vessel to sail all the way around the world.
15. The crew traded knives and mirrors to the Filipinos for these.
16. _____ means "peaceful."

Henry Hudson

In 1607 Henry Hudson was hired by a trading firm, the Muscovy Company, to lead an expedition to the North Pole to find a passage to the Far East. His son, John, went with him.

For awhile they sailed in good weather. Then the temperature dropped and winds and fog appeared. Hudson was surprised that his path was blocked with ice. He thought that the long hours of sunshine at the Pole would melt the ice.

Sailor James Young sighted Greenland; therefore, Hudson named the cape Young's Cape. They killed a bear on the shore, but the unsalted bear meat caused them to get sick, so they ate fish instead.

When they sailed to the Spitsbergen Islands, they saw hundreds of gray whales. In July the crew encountered a violent storm, and a large piece of ice broke off from an ice mass. This *calving* nearly caused the ship to crash into the ice. The men lowered a rowboat (a shallop) into the water so they could row the ship out of the way. Fortunately, the wind shifted and they avoided disaster. The crew's supplies ran low and the weather got worse so Hudson headed for home. They had come 575 nautical miles from the North Pole. No one had ever been that close to it before.

Although Hudson felt the trip had been a failure, the merchants in the Muscovy Company were pleased. He had made the discovery of thousands of whales, and their blubber could be used to make soap and oil. Hudson became known as the father of English whaling.

On his next journey, he planned to sail around the North Pole to the east instead of straight to the Pole. In April of 1608 the ship, *Hopewell,* left London. In June ice blocked its passage and Hudson tried to steer around it. But the ice began to pack together trapping the ship. Although the ice scraped the hull, Hudson was able to get out into clear waters.

One day in the fog two sailors claimed they saw a mermaid. No one is sure what they saw. As they sailed south, a walrus herd napped on nearby icebergs.

In July the crew sailed up a river, but shallow waters forced them to turn back. Hudson was disappointed, as he thought this would have been the passage for which they were looking.

       FS10131 Explorers

Hudson did not want to go home, but his crew was tired. In fear of mutiny, the explorer relented and returned to England in the fall of 1608.

Another trading firm, the Dutch East India Company from Holland, hired him to find a shortcut. Hudson met with Peter Plancius, a mapmaker, to chart new routes. Hudson was paid 800 guilders to lead the expedition. His contract stated that he must only go east of the North Pole, and not travel by any other route. This time he sailed on the *Half Moon*, a small vessel only 60 feet long. Hudson felt he could more easily steer a smaller ship through the ice.

Captain John Smith of Jamestown, Virginia, was anxious to find a route to the Far East, too. He wrote to Hudson, telling him that Indians had said there was a northern sea that reached the western ocean.

Hudson sailed from Amsterdam on April 4, 1609, with a crew of 20 sailors. When ice blocked the ship's path and the crew looked as though they might mutiny, Hudson read Captain Smith's letter and told the sailors they would be rewarded if they found the Northwest Passage. The sailors agreed, but since Hudson broke his contract with the Dutch East India Company, he would not be paid.

As the crew headed toward America it traveled through several storms. In July they reached what is now Penobscot Bay, Maine. Indians paddled out in canoes to meet them, but the sailors were afraid since they had never seen Indians before. Although Hudson fed the Indians and gave them trinkets to show friendship, the sailors worried they might be killed by the Indians.

While in Maine, they repaired their ship. The Indians continued to be friendly, but the sailors were certain they would be attacked. One morning six sailors stole an Indian canoe for a souvenir. Hudson was not pleased.

They headed south and in September they anchored offshore of an island now named Sandy Hook, New York. Hudson thought this river was the one for which they had been searching. But when the river narrowed, sailors took a shallop ahead. Indians attacked the men in the rowboat killing one sailor and injuring others. However, future encounters with Indians were more friendly. Other Indians invited the men to their camps where they were treated like royalty. Hudson wrote, "The natives are a very good people. For when they saw that I would not remain, they supposed that I was afraid of their bows. And taking the arrows, they broke them in pieces, and threw them into the fire."

Hudson returned the hospitality by inviting the Indians onto the ship. He gave them wine—a new experience for the Indians, for they had never had alcohol before.

Due to Hudson's voyage, years later the merchants were able to trade for fur and lumber along the Hudson River with the Indians.

In 1610 several English merchants joined to give Hudson the ship *Discovery*. After the expedition left England, many fights occurred among the crew members. In those days sailors were superstitious; they thought that quarreling on board ship meant they would have bad luck on their voyage. When they saw Mt. Hekla, a large volcano on Iceland, they were sure they were doomed because evil spirits were said to live in volcanos.

Hudson's navigational skills helped them avoid disaster at Furious Overfalls, a dangerous whirlpool at the entrance of the Hudson Strait. The *Discovery* sailed on through Hudson Bay in spite of storms, ice, and lack of food. The expedition was already behind schedule, and Hudson wanted to keep moving because he thought he was about to enter the Pacific Ocean. One time he forced his crew to sail through a storm instead of just anchoring. This decision cost one sailor his life.

They even sailed through darkness at night. Crew members begged Hudson to stop, but he did not listen. When they hit rocks, it took 12 hours for the sailors to move the ship back into the water. The sailors grew angry at Hudson.

In November they docked for the winter and the ship became frozen in the ice. Sickness, cold weather, lack of food, and bad tempers made them miserable. The seamen were forced to eat moss and frogs.

In June the crew mutinied. They tied up Hudson and made him go in the shallop with five other sailors and Hudson's son, John. Later, the mutineers were attacked by Eskimos, and several seamen were killed. Only eight sailors were alive when they landed in London.

Although search boats were sent out for Hudson, no one ever saw or heard from him again.

► *Suggested Teaching Strategies*

Students can read more about Henry Hudson's voyages. Some sources are *The Story of Henry Hudson, Master Explorer* by Eric Winer (Dell), *Henry Hudson* by Joan Joseph (Watts), and *Builders of America* (Funk & Wagnalls).

1. Have students imagine they can travel back in time. They are transported to a different era and are unprepared for their adventures. Students will write a short story about what happens to them.

2. Have students design a castle complete with a moat, dungeon, gatehouse, and drawbridge.

3. The class can study whales and visit an aquarium. Students may write opinion essays on the moratorium for commercial whaling.

4. Students may discuss the changes that would occur if trading and bartering were to replace our current economic system.

5. During Henry Hudson's voyages, King James VI ruled England. Students may read about England's history and write a biography on one of the kings or queens.

6. Students may create a time line of the rulers of England and important historical events that affected the country.

7. The class will divide into groups, each group acting out a scene between the sailors and Hudson that occurred on one of their expeditions.

8. Students may paint pictures of Hudson meeting with the Indians.

9. Students will chart Hudson's voyages on a map. They can use different colored pens to designate the various expeditions.

10. The class may find pictures of early maps. Students can draw them for a bulletin board called "The New World."

Name _____

THE HIGHLIGHTS OF HENRY HUDSON

After reading about Henry Hudson, circle the correct answer.

1. On Hudson's first expedition, his sailors said they saw
   a. a mirage.
   b. a mermaid.
   c. a tornado.

2. *Calving* refers to
   a. when pieces of ice break off a large ice mass.
   b. the process of lowering a rowboat into the ocean.
   c. using a nautical compass.

3. Hudson's crew
   a. was afraid of the Indians.
   b. liked to trade with the Indians.
   c. destroyed the Indians' arrows.

4. Hudson is known for
   a. discovery of a Northwest Passage.
   b. opening trade in Canada and America with Europe.
   c. discovering Greenland.

5. A *shallop* is
   a. a sea animal.
   b. the ship's main mast.
   c. a rowboat.

6. The Muscovy Company was happy with Hudson's 1607 trip because
   a. they knew he would find the passage soon.
   b. his friendship with the Indians would promote good will.
   c. he had discovered thousands of whales.

7. The seamen thought
   a. evil spirits lurked in volcanos.
   b. mermaids were good luck.
   c. wine would provoke the gods.

8. When Hudson entered the strait later named for him, he thought he would
   a. trade with the Eskimos.
   b. soon enter the Pacific Ocean.
   c. enter the Atlantic Ocean.

Name _____

MUTINY ON THE *DISCOVERY*

In June of 1610, Hudson's men whose nerves were frayed by cold weather, a lack of food, and the ruthless tactics of Hudson, placed him, his son, and other members of his crew into a small boat and sent it out to sea. Hudson and his men were never seen nor heard from again.

While this mutiny is well-noted historically, there have been other mutinies equally important to history. Choose one, research the mutiny and record your findings in the space below. Share your discovery with other members of your class.

Name _____

— HENRY HUDSON —

HUDSON'S HISTORY

Using other books as a reference, write the answer to the following questions in complete sentences.

1. How are icebergs formed?

_____
_____
_____
_____

2. Compare U.S. currency to that of the guilder.

_____
_____
_____
_____

3. In the 1500s and 1600s, spices were rare but in big demand. Why?

_____
_____
_____
_____

4. Who was Sebastian Cabot?

_____
_____
_____
_____

Name _____

SAIL ON

Using the clues below, fill in the correct answers in the crossword grid.

Across

1. Two sailors saw a _____.
2. Hudson sighted thousands of these
4. Northwest _____
6. People used this to make soap and oil.
8. _____Hudson
10. Believe in good or bad luck
12. Sailors thought evil spirits lived in these.
14. Furious _____

Down

1. This firm financed Hudson's first voyage.
2. An animal Hudson saw sleeping on an iceberg
3. _____ Islands
5. Merchants traded for fur and _____ with the Indians.
7. Sailors took an Indian canoe for a

    _____.
9. These people attacked the sailors who had mutinied.
11. Seamen were forced to eat this when food supplies ran low.
13. When ice breaks off of a glacier

HENRY HUDSON

NORTH COUNTRY

Locate the following places on the map. Label with the corresponding number.

1. Hudson Bay
2. Hudson Strait
3. James Bay
4. Delaware
5. Chesapeake Bay
6. Labrador Sea
7. Gulf of St Lawrence

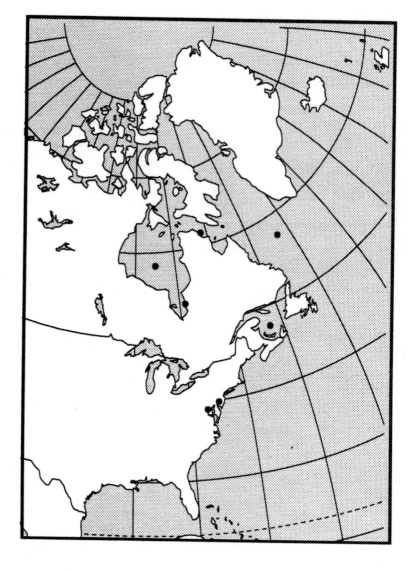

Marco Polo

In 1254 Marco Polo was born in Venice, Italy. Since his father was a merchant, he learned how to handle foreign money, to judge products, and to work with cargo ships.

In 1271 when he was 17, he joined his father and uncle on a trip to China, then referred to as *Cathay*. They sailed from Venice to a port in Palestine. While there they obtained a flask of holy oil before their long journey to the East.

For safety reasons, they traveled by caravan. However, as they approached Hormuz, the group was attacked by the Karaunas, a tribe of bandits in Persia (Iran). The robbers raided during "dust fogs" when the hot winds stirred up the sand and dirt. The Polos had to ride quickly to escape behind the walls of the city.

Once in Hormuz, they discovered that fishing boats were the only vessels available, and they would not be sturdy enough for a long voyage. So the Polos traveled over land. They had to climb high mountains until they reached the Plain of Pamir. This "Roof of the World" was 15,600 miles above sea level.

Marco found large sheep with curling horns which are still known as Ovis Poli, or "Polo's Sheep." For 12 days they hiked in icy temperatures without seeing anyone. The fires they built did not provide much warmth. Marco thought it was because of the cold weather, but it was actually due to the high altitude, where there is less oxygen in the air.

When they reached Turkestan, they used camels and horses to cross the Gobi desert with another caravan. Marco wrote, "This desert is reported to be so long that it would take a year to go from end to end, and at the narrowest point it takes a month to cross it."

The Polos learned about "visions" in which people saw mirages and "spirit voices" which were the sounds of the wind blowing over the dry sands. A month later, they entered China's Tangut province and traveled through Suchow, Sin-Ju, Kalachan, and Tenduc. China's leader, Kublai Khan, sent out an escort to bring the Polos to his palace in Shang-tu. The Polos gave him the holy oil as their gift.

The palace, built with sliced bamboo, was ornate and beautiful. Marco was the first European to report on the Cathayan civilization. The Chinese did not use gold and silver for money. Instead, they used paper. They did not use logs for fuel, but used coal. Marco was amazed with these "stones that burn like logs."

Another surprising aspect of the Chinese culture was the Imperial Post. Messages were delivered by foot for "second class" and on horseback for "first class." "Top priority" meant a message could be delivered 300 miles away within 24 hours. Marco remembered all of these details and wrote about them in his book, *Description of the World*.

Kublai had Marco make several journeys for him as a reporter. Marco's first trip took him to the province of Kara-jang (now Yunnan). In 1272 the King of Mien (Burma) attacked the Mongols in Kara-jang, but they were defeated. Marco saw pagoda towers in Burma that appeared to be made of gold and silver.

Besides the trips on land that he made for China's leader, he went on two sea voyages to the island of Ceylon (now known as Sri Lanka) in 1284. Kublai wanted Marco to buy two Buddhist relics, a tooth and begging bowl of the Buddha. Marco was successful in purchasing them although when he had tried to buy the world's largest ruby, the Buddhist monks would not sell it.

From Ceylon, Marco went to India and found pearl fishers on the Maabar coast. The pearl divers jumped in and dived 60 feet underwater to gather sea oysters. Priests were paid 1 pearl for every 20 found to pray for protection of the divers from shark attacks.

After 17 years, the Polos finally left for home. They sailed from a port in southern China with a fleet of 14 ships. They escorted a princess to Persia. But before Cathayan ships would sail, people would launch a large man-carrying kite. If it soared upwards, the ship would have good luck on the voyage. If it would not climb into the sky, the ship would not sail.

Although the kite flew high, the Polos' trip was extremely dangerous. They landed on Sumatra Island, to wait through five months of bad weather, and had to dig trenches and build strong forts to protect themselves from the fierce cannibal natives. While at sea, every time they came ashore because of storms, robbers would come aboard.

The Polos finally arrived in Venice in 1295. Many people thought they were imposters, until they ripped open the seams of their clothing and showed their hidden jewels.

Marco continued being a merchant and was a commander in the Battle of Curzola in 1298. Defeated by the Genoese, he was taken prisoner. While in prison, he dictated his book to a fellow prisoner. *Description of the World*, also known as *Travels*, was published after he was released from prison in 1299.

His book was popular during the Middle Ages and very important to the history of the world. Columbus was so inspired by reading it, he decided to try to reach Cathay. However, when he sailed west across the Atlantic, he found America.

On Marco Polo's deathbed, a friend told him to admit he made up the stories in his book. Marco refused and said, "I never told half of what I saw!"

► *Suggested Teaching Strategies*

Students can read more about Marco Polo. Some sources are *Marco Polo: Voyager to the Orient* by Carol Greene (Childrens Press), *The Travels of Marco Polo* by Richard Humble (Franklin Watts), and *The Travels of Marco Polo* by Mike Rosen (Bookwright Press).

1. Throughout world history, economics has not always involved currency. Students can act out a scene of trading or bartering.

2. Students may make a time line of the Chinese dynasties and use drawings to symbolize the art produced during the various eras.

3. The Great Wall of China is the largest wall structure man has ever built. The class can create a small three-dimensional model of the wall.

4. Have students read about one of the following topics: Kublai Khan, the Song Dynasty, or Buddhism. Then they can outline important facts about their subject.

5. Students may imagine they are imprisoned for months in a bare cell without modern conveniences. Have them write about what they would do for education and entertainment. They can be creative and make up games and activities to occupy themselves.

6. Using a fine-point pen, students may recreate some of the characters in the Chinese alphabet.

7. More people live in China than in any other country in the world. Students may write an opinion essay on government-regulated population control.

8. Landscapes were a favorite topic in Chinese painting. Students may paint a familiar landscape using watercolors.

9. Marco Polo's *Description of the World* inspired Sir Francis Drake, Vasco da Gama, and Christopher Columbus. Students may write a report on what these men explored and the effects of their explorations on the rest of the world.

10. Students may decorate a bulletin board with a collage representing Marco Polo's adventures.

Name _____

— Marco Polo —

VOYAGE TO THE ORIENT

After reading about Marco Polo, circle the correct answer.

1. As a gift for China's leader, the Polos gave him
   a. Italian lira.
   b. pearls.
   c. holy oil.

2. The Plain of Pamir is
   a. the lowest point in the Gobi Desert.
   b. over 15,000 miles above sea level.
   c. China's grassland region.

3. The Polos stayed in China
   a. 15 years.
   b. 3 years.
   c. 17 years.

4. Before the ships in China would sail
   a. people would launch a kite to see if it would fly.
   b. people would sprinkle holy oil over the sails as a blessing.
   c. people would place a Buddha at the ship's stern.

5. Marco visited Ceylon to
   a. purchase religious relics.
   b. explore the island territory.
   c. make friends with the natives and report back to Kublai.

6. Cathay was the European term for
   a. a merchant ship.
   b. China.
   c. Ceylon.

7. Karaunas were
   a. natives of Ceylon.
   b. bandits in Persia.
   c. warriors of Egypt.

8. The fires the Polos set while on "The Roof of the World" would not provide much warmth because
   a. there was not enough oxygen in the air.
   b. the weather was too cold.
   c. they did not have any coal left.

MARCO POLO

TRAVEL TO CATHAY

Using encyclopedias or other books for reference, fill in the blanks with true or false. If the answer is false, write a correct version of the sentence in the space above it.

_____ 1. The capital of China is Hong Kong.

_____ 2. Mt. Everest is China's highest mountain.

_____ 3. The sea north of Taiwan is the South China Sea.

_____ 4. The island south of India used to be called Ceylon. It is now called Sri Lanka.

_____ 5. China borders eight other countries.

_____ 6. Taipei is the capital of Taiwan.

_____ 7. The country west of 80° E is Japan.

_____ 8. Asia is bordered by three oceans: the Arctic, the Pacific, and the Indian Ocean.

_____ 9. The Bay of Bengal borders both China and Vietnam.

_____10. The Formosa Strait lies between Taiwan and mainland China.

─ MARCO POLO ─
MARCO'S JOURNEY

Using other resources, answer the following questions with complete sentences.

1. Explain why fires do not burn well at high elevations.

   _____

   _____

   _____

   _____

2. Describe these major religions of China:
   Confucianism

   _____

   _____

   _____

   Taoism

   _____

   _____

   _____

   Buddhism

   _____

   _____

   _____

3. Who was Genghis Khan?

   _____

   _____

   _____

   _____

_____ MARCO POLO _____

DESCRIPTION OF THE WORLD

Using the clues below, fill in the correct answers in the crossword grid.

Across

1. The God in Buddhism
3. A tribe of bandits in southern Persia
6. The _____ of Pamir
7. Marco bought the Buddha's _____ from Buddhist monks in Ceylon.
9. _____ Desert
10. The Polos gave this as a gift to Kublai Khan.
12. A large group of merchants who traveled together for safety
13. Marco Polo wrote the book, _____ of the World.
16. Marco was unable to buy the world's largest _____ from the monks.
17. The Polos built forts on the Sumatra Island to protect themselves from these people.

Down

2. A succession of rulers
3. The Polos met this emperor of China
4. Another name for Burma
5. Marco _____
8. The Chinese used this as fuel
11. A Chinese temple
12. European name for China in the Middle Ages
14. Marco observed _____ fishing on the Maabar coast of India.
15. Robbers

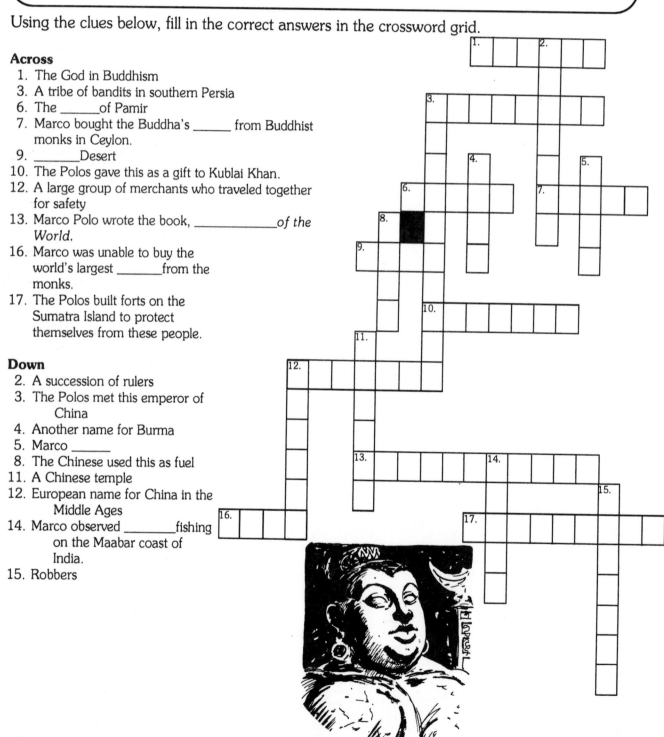

_____ *MARCO POLO* _____

EASTWARD HO!

Locate the following places on the map. Label with the corresponding number.

1. Venice
2. Acre (port in Palestine)
3. Persia (Iran)
4. Hormuz
5. Plain of Pamir
6. Gobi Desert
7. Ceylon (now Sri Lanka)
8. Kara-jang
9. Burma (Mien)
10. Zaiton

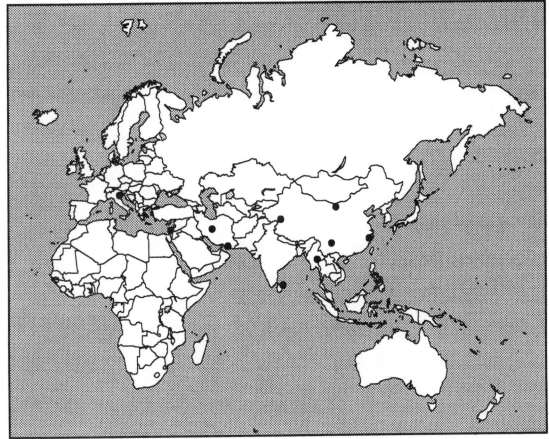

Jacques
Cousteau

Jacques Cousteau was born in France in 1910. As a child, he had two early loves: water and machines. He spent much of his time swimming. At age 11 he built a model crane, and at 13, he constructed a battery-operated car. Jacques also saved his own money for a movie camera and made films.

Later he said, "My films weren't much good. What I liked was taking the camera apart and developing my own film."

In 1930 he attended the French Naval Academy. After graduation he became an officer in the French Navy and would have become a pilot, but he broke both of his arms in a car accident. After months of therapy, he could finally move his fingers.

Swimming helped strengthen his arms. It was then that Cousteau decided to spend his life exploring underwater. In 1939 he was exploring the seas of Africa when he nearly drowned in an underwater cave. While diving he found an ocean floor with holes in it. Sticking his head through a hole, he discovered the floor to be a platform on columns. The actual bottom of the sea was three feet deeper. Sunlight streamed through another hole.

He returned to the surface for air. In his next dive he moved through the hole, and during the third dive he entered the first hole and tried to leave through a second hole. But the second hole was too narrow and Cousteau did not have enough oxygen left in his lungs to swim back to the entrance. Fortunately, he found a third hole and escaped through it.

"That dive taught me a lot," he said. "I didn't check the escape hole before hand . . . free divers had to have breathing apparatus so they would not be trapped by time."

As Cousteau searched for a compressed air lung, he tried helmet diving, but he hated the heavy suits. The lines leading to the surface did not give him enough freedom. So he and engineer Emile Gagnan created the aqualung, a breathing machine with chambers. When a diver inhales, the air comes from one chamber; exhaled air is released into the second chamber.

When World War II began, Cousteau became a spy for the Allies. On one adventure, he dressed up as an enemy soldier, entered Italian headquarters to open a safe, and used a miniature camera to copy a code book and other secret papers.

After the war Cousteau started the Undersea Research Group for divers and oceanographers. The diving group traveled on his ship, the *Calypso*.

In 1952 Cousteau and his diving partners, Philippe Tailliez and Frederic Dumas, joined with archeologist Fernand Benoit to explore an ancient wreck off Grand Congloue Island. They retrieved artifacts dating back to the third century B.C. The National Geographic Society and the French government gave them money and supplies, and Cousteau hired divers and engineers to help with the project. Since the sunken ship was under the island, they dived from a rock they named Port Calypso.

Cousteau and his crew brought up amphoras (jars made of baked clay that were used to carry water, food, and oil), bronze nails, lead plates, stone pots, and the ship's anchor. Divers took photographs and measurements. Film director, Louis Malle, made a movie of their expedition.

In the Indian Ocean, they took films of Assumption Reef, where they captured the beauty of corals and fish on film. Although most of the fish ignored the divers, one grouper followed them around like a dog. The divers nicknamed the fish Ulysses and fed him. They even petted his fins and scratched his head! He was so friendly, he ruined several filming scenes by swimming in front of the camera. The divers finally had to put him in an anti-shark cage so they could finish the movie. While in the cage, Ulysses got so much food and attention, that when it came time to release him, he did not want to leave!

On another dive in the Red Sea, Cousteau and his crew discovered a fish 9 feet high and 12 feet long. No one had ever seen anything like it. "He passed a truck on deck and he was as big as the truck," said one diver. This "truckfish" was later identified as a hump-headed wrasse. Until that date, the largest wrasse ever seen had only been three feet long.

Cousteau explored for oil under the sea floor in the Persian Gulf. By using an instrument called a gravity meter, oil can be found under domes or sand layers. The gravity meter measured the gravity of the earth. If the gravity was different, oil could be located under the sand. Cousteau and his men discovered 400 oil stations on their trip.

While sailing in the Persian Gulf, thousands of porpoises swam along the ship. Many of them jumped 12 feet into the air. Afer two hours of performing, they swam out into the Arabian Sea.

On an expedition in the Indian Ocean, nine whales swam with the *Calypso*. One whale bumped into it and injured himself seriously. He let out shrill squeaks. Moments later, whales came from all around. (The crew counted 27 whales in all.) Unfortunately, the ship's propeller blades had seriously hurt the whale, so the crew shot it to put it out of its misery.

Immediately, sharks circled the whale. Cousteau filmed the shark attack from an anti-shark cage, which was lowered into the ocean. This film helped divers learn more about their enemies, the sharks. The scenes became part of the movie, *The Silent World*.

His concern for the ocean extended beyond his own interest into conservation. In 1960 Cousteau prevented France from dumping radioactive waste into the Mediterranean Sea. His exploration and research have allowed new developments in technologies for environmental protection.

In 1962 Cousteau wanted to find out whether people could live on the bottom of the sea. So he made an underwater home called Conshelf I. Two men lived in this barrel-shaped dwelling for one week at 33 feet deep. Conshelf II and III were larger and went deeper.

During the 1960s and 1970s, he had his own television series, *The Undersea World of Jacques Cousteau*, and in 1974 he began the Cousteau Society to protect oceans. In 1985 President Reagan awarded him the Medal of Freedom. Cousteau has authored *The Silent World, The Living Sea,* and *World Without Sun*. His movies have won three Academy Awards.

Over the years, Cousteau has developed many inventions. Besides the aqualung and the undersea habitats, he has helped create the first deep-sea cameras, the first small submarine for ocean research (the "Diving Saucer"), and a wind-propulsion system for ships (the Turbosail).

"I wonder why we are dreaming of space when we know nothing about what is under our feet inside the earth," said Cousteau.

▶ *Suggested Teaching Strategies*

For further research, students can read *Undersea Explorer* by James Dugan (Harper), *Life in the Deep Sea* by Isaac Asimov (Walker), and *Into the Unknown* written and published by The National Geographic Society.

1. Have students draw pictures of Cousteau's aqualung. They can label the parts and in one paragraph, explain how it works.

2. Using papier-mache or clay, students may create models of the ocean floor's topography and sea life.

3. Students will read about ancient civilizations and write scenes showing what life was like in ancient Egypt, Greece, or the ancient city of Rome. In small groups, students will then act out their scenes for the class.

4. Using pencils, students will sketch a map of the world and label oceans and seas. As a fun way to test their memories, divide the class into two groups. With a blank world map drawn on the chalkboard, teams take turns writing down the names of bodies of water. One point is given for each correct answer.

5. Have students make diagrams of the *Calypso* and her underwater equipment.

6. Students may investigate what the Cousteau Society and The American Oceans Campaign do to help our oceans. Why are the oceans in trouble? Students may write essays about what we can do to protect our seas.

7. Turn your classroom's clock back in time. The class may throw a 1950s party! Students may discover the fads, fashion, music, and food popular during that era; and make snacks and decorations; and play games to fit the 1950s theme.

8. Oil is a large ocean polluter. After researching the need for oil and some major oil spills, students may debate ocean oil drilling.

9. Have students imagine they are divers exploring sunken ships and write journal entries describing what they see. What does finding a past tragedy make them think and feel?

10. Students may design bulletin boards using paintings and drawings they have made of a variety of sea life.

JACQUES COUSTEAU

THE SILENT WORLD

After reading about Jacques Cousteau, circle the correct answer.

1. Jacques Cousteau planned on becoming a
   a. movie producer.
   b. professional swimmer.
   c. pilot.

2. Cousteau wanted to stay underwater for longer periods of time so he
   a. used a helmet with lines leading to the surface.
   b. did lung exercises to improve his lung capacity.
   c. invented the aqualung.

3. During World War II, he
   a. was a spy.
   b. fought in the army.
   c. was a pilot for the French airforce.

4. Cousteau found a ship that was from
   a. the third century A.D.
   b. the third century B.C.
   c. the 1600s.

5. The crew discovered *amphoras*, which are
   a. tiny diatom skeletons.
   b. Roman writings on stoneware.
   c. jars made of baked clay.

6. Conshelf I was an
   a. experimental breathing apparatus.
   b. a house under the sea.
   c. an advanced aqualung regulator.

7. The divers found _____oil stations in the Persian Gulf.
   a. 400
   b. 100
   c. over 500

8. Louis Malle
   a. was the archeologist who helped explore the ancient wreck.
   b. directed films of their dives.
   c. authored *The Silent World* with Cousteau.

76

JACQUES COUSTEAU

EXPLORE THE DEPTHS BELOW

Write a paragraph answering each of the following questions. Use your library to research the answers.

1. How does sonar help navigation?

   _____

   _____

   _____

   _____

2. How are driftnets stripmining the oceans?

   _____

   _____

   _____

   _____

3. What are some important diving milestones in history?

   _____

   _____

   _____

   _____

Name _____

UNDERWATER WONDERS

Using other books to help you, find the correct answers to this matching exercise. Place the letter in the blank beside the correct answer.

___ 1. Fritz Haber

___ 2. zooplankton

___ 3. thermocline

___ 4. eupholic zone

___ 5. Otto F. Muller

___ 6. estuary

___ 7. continental margin

___ 8. James Clark Ross

___ 9. abyssal plain

___ 10. Jacques Piccard

a. mouth of a river where the salt water tide meets the fresh water current

b. flat sea floor between an ocean ridge and a continental slope

c. designed and boarded a bathyscaphe, the *Trieste*, which sunk 13 1/2 miles to the bottom of the ocean in 1960.

d. chemist who first used sonar from his ship

e. microscopic animal life

f. top 250 feet of the ocean, where sunlight penetrates

g. a layer of water through which the temperature falls from the warmer surface to the cooler deep water

h. first explorer to try to discover the depth of the ocean

i. biologist who made a dredge in the 1770s to bring ocean life to the surface

j. where a continent and ocean basin meet

Name ______________________________

JACQUES COUSTEAU

ANOTHER WORLD

Write a paragraph or two on the following ideas.

1. After looking at photographs of coral reefs, use sensory imagery to describe them.

____
____
____
____

2. You are the fish Ulysses. Write about your experiences with Cousteau and his divers.

____
____
____
____

3. Make up a haiku (poem without rhyme) on the theme of marine life.

Line 1 ______________________
five syllables

Line 2 ______________________
seven syllables

Line 3 ______________________
five syllables

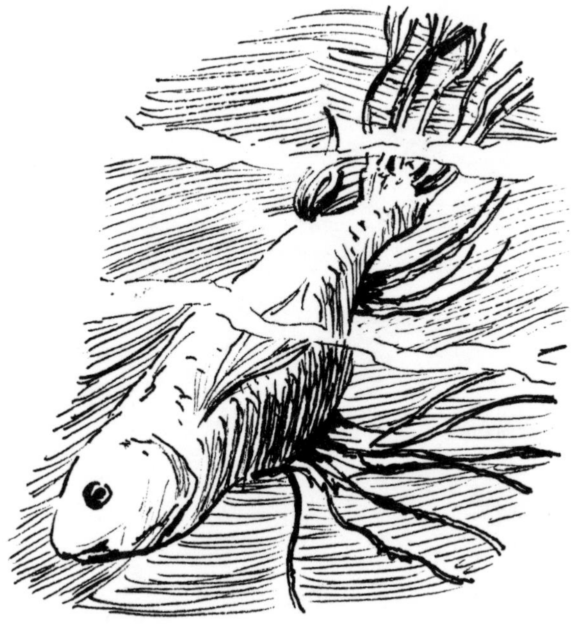

JACQUES COUSTEAU

OCEAN GEOLOGY

Using other books for research, label the ocean basin below.

1. abyssal plain
2. mountain range
3. continental shelf
4. continental slope
5. ocean ridge

6. ocean trench
7. crust
8. inner lithosphere
9. aesthenosphere (outer mantle)

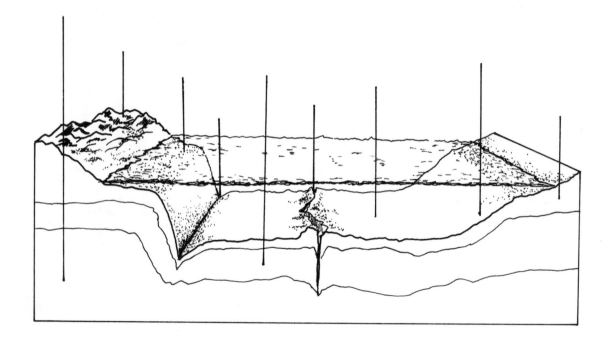

EDUCATIONAL MATERIALS FOR TEACHERS

Here are some addresses of sources of free environmental or geographic information.

National Geographic Society
1145 17th Street NW
Washington, DC 20036
Free Geography Materials

American Oceans Campaign
725 Arizona Avenue, Suite 102
Santa Monica, CA 90401
Free Materials for Children

Project WILD
US Fish and Wildlife Service
Division of Policy and Directives Management
18th and C Streets NW
Washington, DC 20240
Free Aquatic Educational Activity Guide

ERIC Clearinghouse for Science, Mathematics, and
  Environmental Education
1929 Kenny Rd
Columbus, OH 43210-1080
Environmental Information

The Cousteau Society
870 Greenbrier Circle Suite 402
Chesapeake, VA 23320-2641
Materials and Magazines on Oceans

The Marine Mammal Center
Marin Headlands
GGNRA
Sausalito, CA 94965
Marine Mammmal Activity and Curriculum Guide

Name _____

UNDER THE SEA

Using the clues below, fill in the correct answers in the crossword grid.

Across

1. Cousteau was a spy in the _____.
3. The Silent _____
4. Underwater explorer
5. Cousteau received a Medal of _____.
8. This meter helped divers find oil.
10. The fish who acted like a pet
11. Large aquatic mammals
12. Ancient clay jars
14. The gulf where Cousteau found oil
15. Man-made home undersea

Down

2. Breathing machine for divers
3. A huge fish
6. Cousteau won Academy Awards for these.
7. Cousteau's ship
9. Coral _____
13. They jumped 12 feet into the air.

Charles Darwin

Charles Darwin was born in England in 1809. As a child, he loved nature. He went on long walks where he collected stones and insects and studied plants and animals. Since his father and grandfather were doctors, everyone expected him to become one, too. At age 16, he enrolled in medical school but found that he hated to see blood and suffering. So he attended Cambridge University to become a minister. While there, he collected insects and became friends with a professor of botany. This professor introduced him to Captain Robert Fitzroy of the Royal Navy.

Captain Fitzroy needed a naturalist to come with him on a five-year sailing journey. The Captain planned to map the coast of South America and take measurements around the world. Darwin was thrilled to accompany him and the 72-man crew. He took a compass, a book on taxidermy, binoculars, a magnifying glass, and jars of spirits in which to preserve specimens.

They left England in December 1831. Unfortunately, Darwin was seasick the entire time they were sailing. He was relieved to visit the Canary and the Cape Verde Islands.

When he explored the tropical forests of Brazil, he discovered a fish that blew itself up with water and air. When it was in danger, it squirted water at its enemies. This fish, a Diodon, could eat its way out of a shark and kill it.

The crew stayed in Brazil several months. Although Darwin enjoyed exploring forests and visiting a coffee-growing plantation, he was upset to see that slavery was a common practice.

The *Beagle* sailed down the coast to Montevideo, where Darwin packed his collection of specimens to send to England. He had 50 different types of birds, nine kinds of snakes, and many other reptiles.

For two years the *Beagle* traveled along the coast of South America, while the crew made maps and surveyed. Darwin spent some time aboard the ship and some on land.

On one land excursion, he rode horseback 400 miles over the Pampas Plains to Buenos Aires with gauchos, or cowboys. The gauchos wore tall white boots, wide trousers, and red sashes. They used the lasso and the bola to herd their cattle. One time, one end of Darwin's

FS10131 Explorers

bola got caught on a bush and the other end wound around his horse's hind legs. Darwin wrote, "The gauchos roared with laughter; they cried out that they had seen every sort of animal caught, but had never before seen a man caught by himself."

In Punta Alta Darwin found large fossilized skeletons of a megatherium, a mastodon, and a glyptodont. He discovered a fossilized tooth of a horse in Santa Fe. This interested him, since when the Spanish came to South America in 1535, horses were nonexistent.

During his explorations, the Spanish were at war with the South American Indians. Darwin felt sorry for the Indians, since the Spanish were ruining their way of life. He did not think the Indians would survive. He wrote, "It is melancholy to trace how the Indians have given way before the Spanish invaders."

Darwin and the crew sailed to Tierra del Fuego, the tip of South America, in 1832 and again in 1834. On their first visit they met native Fuegians who painted their faces black and red with white circles around their eyes. The natives lived in shelters made out of tree branches and slept on the cold, wet ground. They did not wear clothes and sometimes starved in the winter.

In 1834 the *Beagle* sailed up the western coast of South America to Valparaiso, Chile. The warm climate was a relief after the miserable weather of Tierra del Fuego. Darwin found gold and copper mines but noticed the miners had poor working conditions. The miners had to carry 200 pounds of rock up notches in tree trunks across the mine shafts.

In February 1835, the expedition sailed to Concepcion, where a terrible earthquake had completely destroyed the city and harbor. Many people were able to escape their homes, so only 100 people were killed out of 1,000 villagers. Darwin studied the earthquake's effect on the land. He found that the land had risen two or three feet with the quake.

In March Darwin crossed the Cordillera range of the Andes mountains. He found fossilized shells, which meant that at one time, the mountains had been under the ocean. Darwin agreed with British geologist, Charles Lyell, who felt that the level of the earth had changed greatly over millions of years. When Darwin discovered fir trees that had turned to stone, he knew this was more evidence to prove Lyell's theory.

In September of 1835, the *Beagle* sailed to the Galapagos Islands. When Darwin saw the black rocks of the islands, he knew they had been underwater volcanos. On the islands, he rode on 300-pound tortoises, found three-foot sea-living lizards, and 33 types of finches. Their physical characteristics were not typical of finches which lived elsewhere. Their beaks were different on each island, depending upon the food available. One island had an abundance of nuts, so the finches had sturdy, thick beaks.

Another island had berries, so the beaks were rounder. On an island where seeds were available, the beaks were smaller and more pointed. He realized this showed that animals adapt to their living conditions and gradually change over time. He named this process "natural selection" or "survival of the fittest." The fittest were not the strongest–they were the most suited to their habitat. He believed that "natural selection" allowed the fittest beings to live and reproduce.

The *Beagle* sailed to Tahiti and island natives guided Darwin over mountains. In New Zealand Darwin was angry that the people were not compassionate to their slaves. In Australia Darwin was disappointed that there were few animals to see. He met aborigines and wrote, "Wherever the European has trod, death seems to pursue the aboriginal."

On Keeling Island, Darwin found coconut-eating crab and studied the coral reefs. The crew became homesick and returned to England on October 2, 1836, nearly five years after they had begun their journey.

After Darwin's return, he wrote *Journal of the Voyage of "The Beagle,"* published in 1839. He married his cousin Emma and they had 10 children. His book, *On the Origin of Species* is considered his most important work. Published in 1859, it was sold out on the first day of its sale! In his book, *The Descent of Man,* published in 1871, he discussed his belief that all species evolved from common ancestors.

His revolutionary ideas were controversial, for he believed the world adapted over time while people in Victorian England had always believed that God had created a perfect world in six days, so there would never be a need for change.

After Darwin's death in 1882, his ideas became respected. His explorations on the *Beagle* allowed him to develop the theory of evolution, which is considered to be one of the greatest discoveries of science.

▶ Suggested Teaching Strategies

For further research, students can read *The Voyage of "The Beagle,"* by Kate Hyndley (Bookwright Press), *"The Beagle" and Mr. Flycatcher* by Robert Quackenbush (Prentice-Hall), and *The Voyage of "The Beagle"* by Charles Darwin (Doubleday).

1. Have students draw a diagram of Darwin's Theory of Evolution. (Example: Draw figures for Pliopithecus, Proconsul, Rama-pithecus, Australopithecus, Homo Erectus, and Cro Magnon Man.)

2. Students may wish to write essays about how animals adapt to their habitats.

3. Have students act as if they are travel agents and plan a trip to one of the places Darwin explored. They can create an itinerary as well as design a travel poster advertising the adventure.

4. Have a Natural History Fair! Students may start their own collection of shells, rocks, or insects and read books to become authorities on their subject. Students may bring their collections to arrange in a display for a class or school Natural History Fair.

5. In the United States, "Tippecanoe and Tyler too" and "Remember the Alamo" were phrases used during the 1830s. Students may write about the significance of one of these sayings.

6. Have students paint a picture of an animal Darwin found on his travels.

7. The crew of the *Beagle* nicknamed Darwin "Mr. Flycatcher." Students will write journal entries by a member of the crew observing Darwin.

8. Have students list five ways to *prepare* for an earthquake, five things to do *during* a quake, and five things to do *after* an earthquake. A class discussion may follow.

9. Students may make a bar graph of earthquakes throughout history. They can include dates, places, Richter scale measurements, and property damage or loss of life.

10. Students may design a bulletin board called "Beat the Quake!"

Name _____

— CHARLES DARWIN —

DARWIN'S LEGACY

After reading about Charles Darwin, circle the correct answer.

1. Darwin discovered the Diodon, a
   - a. finch with a hard beak for eating nuts.
   - b. fish that sprayed water at its enemies.
   - c. fossilized skeleton.

2. What did Darwin find in Punta Ata?
   - a. gauchos
   - b. a fossilized tortoise
   - c. a fossilized horse tooth

3. Darwin figured that the Andes Mountains had
   - a. once been underwater because he found fossilized shells.
   - b. black rocks which meant they had been volcanic.
   - c. sea-living lizards living in the mountains.

4. His "survival of the fittest" meant
   - a. only the strongest creatures would survive.
   - b. population control.
   - c. creatures adapt to their living conditions to exist.

5. As a child, Darwin
   - a. wanted to become a doctor like his father.
   - b. collected stones.
   - c. knew he would become a naturalist.

6. Darwin met Captain Fitzroy because
   - a. his botany professor introduced them.
   - b. he was a professor at Cambridge.
   - c. he was his father's friend.

7. The *Beagle's* journey lasted from
   - a. 1713-1718.
   - b. 1863-1868.
   - c. 1831-1836.

8. Lyell's theory was that
   - a. slavery should be abolished.
   - b. the level of the earth changed over time.
   - c. earth remained unchanged since creation.

         FS10131 Explorers

CHARLES DARWIN

THE NATURAL NATURALIST

Answer each of the following questions in complete sentences. Use the article on Darwin and other books in your library to help you in your research.

1. Cite examples of Darwin's compassion for people.

   _____
   _____
   _____
   _____

2. How is coral made?

   _____
   _____
   _____
   _____

3. Describe the gaucho's lasso and the bola.

   _____
   _____
   _____
   _____

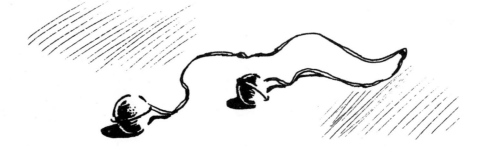

Name _____

EXPLORE HISTORY

This is a time line of events that occurred while Darwin explored on the *Beagle*. Choose one of these historical topics and write a report organizing your thoughts on index cards. Include footnotes and a bibliography of your resources.

1832   North East Antislavery Society founded.
        The Black Hawk War begins.
1833   Andrew Jackson begins second term.
        Tax supported public library established in New Hampshire.
1834   Cyrus McCormick patents reaping machine.
1835   Samuel Colt patents revolver.
1836   Texas declares independence from Mexico.
        The Alamo is captured.
        Samuel Morse builds telegraph.

Cover Darwin's explorations as if you are a newspaper reporter. Choose one adventure on this partial time line of the *Beagle's* journey and create newspaper headlines, articles, a cartoon, an editorial column, and letters to the editor.

    "The Beagle" and its crew . . .
    December 27, 1831   leave from England.
    January 16, 1832   land on Cape Verde Island.
    April 5, 1832   explore Rio De Janeiro.
    July 23, 1832   land at Montevideo.
    February 20, 1835   are in an earthquake at Valdivia.
    September 16, 1835   visit the Galapagos Islands.
    November 15, 1835   tour Tahiti.
    December 21, 1835   explore New Zealand.
    October 2, 1836   land at Falmouth.

Name _____

_____ CHARLES DARWIN _____

EVOLUTION OF THE MIND

1. Have you ever been in an earthquake or natural disaster? Describe the after-effects of a disaster.

   _____

   _____

   _____

2. Using fruit which would be found in the tropics, experiment, and create your own tasty fruit drink! Write your recipe, using exact ingredients and amounts. Make certain your directions are clear.

   _____

   _____

   _____

3. Write a cinquain poem about an animal that Darwin saw on his expedition.

   Line 1 _____
   one word - can be the title

   Line 2 _____
   two words - describing title

   Line 3 _____
   three words - an action

   Line 4 _____
   four words - a feeling

   Line 5 _____
   one word - about the title

Name _____

WHICH ANIMALS LIVE WHERE?

Using other books to help you, find the correct answer in this matching exercise. Place the letter in the blank beside the correct answer.

_____ 1. saiga

_____ 2. yak

_____ 3. manatee

_____ 4. chinchilla

_____ 5. spider monkey

_____ 6. musk ox

_____ 7. kudu

_____ 8. pronghorn

_____ 9. flying squirrel

_____10. jaguar

a. high mountains
b. grasslands
c. temperate forest
d. tropical forest
e. desert
f. polar regions
g. oceans

CHARLES DARWIN

SURVIVAL OF THE FITTEST

Using the clues below, fill in the correct answers in the crossword grid.

Across

3. Means giant tortoise in Spanish
5. field glasses
6. Captain who led the expedition
7. sample
8. water spraying fish
10. the ship Darwin sailed upon
13. large turtle
14. small animals that form coral
15. South American cowboys
16. what people gather on the beach

Down

1. navigational instrument shows direction
2. stuffing and mounting animals
4. native of Australia
6. petrified remains
9. birds Darwin studied
11. natural disaster
12. geologist Charles _____

─── CHARLES DARWIN ───

DARWINIAN EXPLORATIONS

12. geologist Charles _____

Put the appropriate numbers of the places Darwin explored next to the dots on the map.

1. Canary Islands	4. Cape Verde Islands	7. Keeling Island
2. Valparaiso	5. Tahiti	8. Tierra del Fuego
3. Galapagos Islands	6. Buenos Aires	9. Sydney

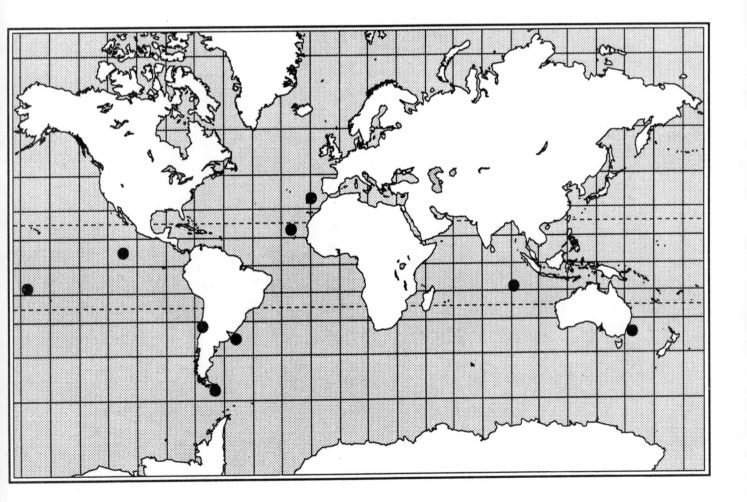

▶ Suggested Teaching Strategies

1. Students may choose the most important facts in the explorers' lives to create a picture book for each explorer. After the text is written, students include pictures to illustrate the action. Then, the class can share the books with children in the primary grades.

2. Some say the journey to the moon was a propaganda stunt and a waste of taxpayers' money and technology. Have students debate this question and then write their views in opinion essays.

3. Have students make a world map and chart the routes of these explorers: Bartolomeu Dias, Sir Richard Burton, Louis Jollie, Leif Ericson, and Alexander the Great.

4. Have students choose one of those explorers to study. Using the library, they can create a bibiliography on what has been written about their explorer. Students may write a synopsis about his life and accomplishments.

5. Have a class discussion on how methods of exploration have changed through history.

6. Students may make a time line of inventions in history that have aided explorations.

7. It is 20 years from now. Students may wish to role play being the first person to accomplish an action. What will they do? Have students become reporters and write articles about their adventures.

8. Have students make their own crossword puzzles about the explorers listed in activity number three. The class can trade puzzles and use library resources to discover the answers.

9. Students may play "Who Am I?" by assuming the identity of an explorer. The class asks yes/no questions to find out who they are.

10. Students may play the Explorer's Trivia Game. Divide the class into two teams. Cut out the following cards and shuffle them. Award one point for each correct answer. If the first team gives an incorrect answer, the next team is allowed to try for the point. After all the questions have been asked, whoever has the most points is the winner.

EXPLORERS
TRIVIA CARD

Lewis and Clark met the Wanapam Indians. Why was this tribe so unusual?

EXPLORERS
TRIVIA CARD

What was "The Dark Continent"?

EXPLORERS
TRIVIA CARD

The Indians frowned upon the animal meat that Lewis and Clark's crew ate. What was it?

EXPLORERS
TRIVIA CARD

David Livingstone named the Victoria Falls in Africa. After whom were they named?

EXPLORERS
TRIVIA CARD

How much money did the United States pay for the Louisiana Purchase?

EXPLORERS
TRIVIA CARD

What was the name of Livingstone's steamboat?

EXPLORERS
TRIVIA CARD

Who was president when Lewis and Clark made their journey?

EXPLORERS
TRIVIA CARD

While Livingstone was working on a mission in Mabotsa, he nearly died. Why?

Africa Livingstone	**They were head-flatteners.** Lewis and Clark
England's Queen Victoria Livingstone	**They ate dog meat.** Lewis and Clark
Lady Nyasa Livingstone	**15 million dollars** **(about four cents an acre)** Lewis and Clark
A lion attacked him. Livingstone	**Thomas Jefferson** Lewis and Clark

EXPLORERS
TRIVIA CARD

What was the first animal to travel in space?

EXPLORERS
TRIVIA CARD

Captain Cook surveyed the St. Lawrence River during which war?

EXPLORERS
TRIVIA CARD

Who was the first American to orbit the earth?

EXPLORERS
TRIVIA CARD

Where did Cook go to see the passing of Venus between the Earth and Sun?

EXPLORERS
TRIVIA CARD

What was the name of the spacecraft that landed on the moon in 1969?

EXPLORERS
TRIVIA CARD

Cook used the first chronometer. What was a chronometer?

EXPLORERS
TRIVIA CARD

Who were the astronauts that walked on the moon?

EXPLORERS
TRIVIA CARD

What is scurvy?

The Seven Years War Cook	**A dog named Laika** Armstrong
Tahiti Cook	**John Glenn** Armstrong
A ship's clock that timed the voyage and helped the crew calculate their east-west longitude Cook	**Apollo 11** Armstong
During the time of Captain Cook, scurvy was a disease sailors got from lack of nutrition. Symptoms include bleeding gums, blood infections, and loss of appetitie. Cook	**Edwin (Buzz) Aldrin and Neil Armstrong** Armstrong

EXPLORERS
TRIVIA CARD

Which president wished Admiral Peary good luck?

EXPLORERS
TRIVIA CARD

As a child, what did Magellan do?

EXPLORERS
TRIVIA CARD

To what does "The Big Lead" refer?

EXPLORERS
TRIVIA CARD

What was the Treaty of Tordesillas?

EXPLORERS
TRIVIA CARD

When did Peary reach the North Pole?

EXPLORERS
TRIVIA CARD

What was the name of the first ship to sail all the way around the world?

EXPLORERS
TRIVIA CARD

Who was the man who claimed he reached the North Pole before Peary?

EXPLORERS
TRIVIA CARD

Magellan and his crew were the first white men to see two types of animals. What were they?

He was a page for King John of Portugal. **Magellan**	**Theodore Roosevelt** **Peary**
An agreement signed between Portugal and Spain to share newly discovered lands **Magellan**	A large break in the ice **Peary**
The *Victoria* **Magellan**	**1909** **Peary**
Penguins and seals **Magellan**	**Dr. Frederick Cook** **Peary**

EXPLORERS
TRIVIA CARD

Where was Marco Polo born?

EXPLORERS
TRIVIA CARD

What happened to Henry Hudson?

EXPLORERS
TRIVIA CARD

What was called the "Roof of the World"?

EXPLORERS
TRIVIA CARD

What was the name of the volcano Hudson's crew saw?

EXPLORERS
TRIVIA CARD

What animal is named for Marco Polo?

EXPLORERS
TRIVIA CARD

What was the name of the first trading company that hired Hudson to find a route to the Far East?

EXPLORERS
TRIVIA CARD

What was the name of the desert Polo had to cross?

EXPLORERS
TRIVIA CARD

What is "calving"?

His crew tied him up and put him in a shallop. He was never heard from again. Hudson	Venice, Italy Polo
Mount Hekla Hudson	The Plain of Pamir Polo
The Muscovy Company Hudson	Sheep Polo
When a large piece of ice breaks off from an ice mass Hudson	The Gobi Desert Polo

EXPLORERS
TRIVIA CARD

What did Emile Gagnan and Jacques Cousteau invent?

EXPLORERS
TRIVIA CARD

What was the name of Darwin's ship?

EXPLORERS
TRIVIA CARD

What did Cousteau do during the war?

EXPLORERS
TRIVIA CARD

What were South American cowboys called?

EXPLORERS
TRIVIA CARD

What is an amphora?

EXPLORERS
TRIVIA CARD

In what year did the devastating earthquake in Concepcion, Chile, occur?

EXPLORERS
TRIVIA CARD

What was the name of Cousteau's first underwater home?

EXPLORERS
TRIVIA CARD

Who was the captain of Darwin's expedition?

FS10131 Explorers

The *Beagle* Darwin	The aqualung Cousteau
Gauchos Darwin	Became a spy for the Allies Cousteau
1835 Darwin	A clay jar from ancient civilizations Cousteau
Captain Robert Fitzroy Darwin	Conshelf 1 Cousteau

ANSWER KEY

Lewis and Clark

The Trail
Page 5
1. b
2. c
3. b
4. a
5. c
6. a
7. a
8. c

Frontier Folks
Page 6
1. b
2. f
3. a
4. e
5. j
6. h
7. g
8. i
9. d
10. c

Tribes Along the Trail
Page 7
1. Colonel George A. Custer led his troops against the Sioux Indians.
2. The Arikara Indians used willow branches and straw to make round lodges 30 to 40 feet wide. Many families and their horses lived in one dwelling.
3. The Shoshoni Indians gave them horses so the crew could travel in the mountains.
4. The Wanapam Indians pressed their babies' heads between boards to flatten the front of the skull, nose, and forehead.
5. The Chinook Indians tried to steal *Seaman* from Lewis and Clark.
6. *Nez Perce* is a French word which means "pierced nose." These Indians put ornaments such as shells and rings through holes in their noses.
7. The Mandans lived in western North Dakota along the Missouri River.

The Trail to the West
Page 8

David Livingstone

Livingstone's Life
Page 14
1. b
2. a
3. c
4. b
5. b
6. c
7. a
8. c

Out of Africa
Page 15
1. b
2. c
3. h
4. j
5. d
6. e
7. n
8. i
9. l
10. o
11. m
12. g
13. f
14. k
15. a

African Safari
Page 16
1. T
2. F   The southern tip of Africa is called the Cape of Good Hope. Cape Horn is the southern tip of South America.
3. F   The Nile River flows north into the Mediterranean Sea.
4. T
5. F   Africa's highest peak is Mt. Kilimanjaro.
6. F   Africa is larger than the United States.

7. T
8. T
9. F   Antananarivo is the capital of Madagascar. Libya's capital is Tripoli.
10. F   Ethiopia's capital is Addis Ababa. Somalia's capital is Mogadishu.

The Dark Continent
Page 17
1. Madagascar
2. Nile
3. Sahara
4. Addis Ababa
5. Cairo
6. Zambezi
7. Victoria Lake
8. Mt Kilimanjaro

Neil Armstrong

Journey to the Moon
Page 22
1. c
2. a
3. a
4. c
5. c
6. b
7. a
8. c

Space Facts
Page 23
1. T
2. T
3. F   The spacecraft was called *Apollo*, and the rocket was name Saturn.
4. F   They fell into the Atlantic Ocean.
5. T
6. T
7. F   Mars is nicknamed the Red Planet.
8. F   Venus is the closest planet to the earth.
9. T
10. F   The Andromeda is a constellation in the northern sky. Within this constellation is the Andromeda galaxy.

Space to Learn
Page 24
1. The big bang theory is the belief that the universe began as a tiny ball and expanded with an explosion that occurred 15 to 20 billion years ago. This theory was developed by George Lemaitre in 1927.
2. A sunspot is a magnetic storm on the sun's surface. It appears darker, as it is a little cooler than the surrounding area.
3. Zero gravity is the condition of weightlessness in space. It happens when the force of gravity is balanced by the speed and power of a moving vehicle.
4. The speed of light is the same everywhere. Mass and energy are interchangeable. Time slows down as one nears the speed of light. This helps to show how gravity bends space and time.
5. Answers will vary.

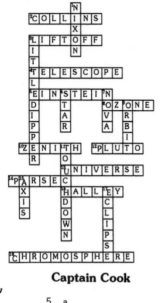

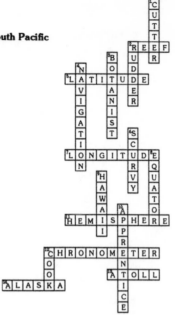

Captain Cook

Cook's Stew   **Page 31**

1. c   5. a
2. a   6. a
3. b   7. b
4. b   8. c

Admiral Peary

The Land of Ice   **Page 39**

1. b   5. c
2. a   6. c
3. c   7. a
4. b   8. b

Exploring   **Page 32**

1. The Seven Years War (or French and Indian War) lasted from 1756-1763. In North America, both French and English colonies wanted to control the fur trade, fishing grounds, and land. The Iroquois Indians allowed British settlers to live in the Ohio River Valley. The French wanted the control over this area, so they built forts. The war broke out in America in 1754 and spread to Europe in 1756.
2. The Maoris were fisherman, hunters, and farmers. They were skilled in carving their wooden homes and canoes with intricate designs. The Maoris pressed their noses together as a form of greeting. They held gatherings called *hui* and danced and sang action songs.
3. A *transit* occurs when one body crosses over another. These movements can be used to measure the size of the solar system. The Transit of Venus is very rare.
4. 1773—Boston Tea Party,
   1774—Paul Revere's ride
   1775—Patrick Henry's speech, "Give me liberty or give me death."
   1775—American Revolution began.
   1776—Nathan Hale executed by the British for spying. 1777—A Treaty of Alliance with France was signed. 1779—Spain enters a war against England.

North to the Pole   **Page 44**

Ferdinand Magellan

Passage to the Pacific   **Page 49**

1. c   5. a
2. a   6. b
3. b   7. a
4. c   8. c

You Are There   **Page 50**

Answers will vary

Who's Who   **Page 51**

1. c   6. a
2. j   7. b
3. f   8. g
4. i   9. e
5. h   10. d

South Seas   **Page 33**

1. T
2. F Honolulu is located on Oahu.
3. T
4. F The small island off the southern coast of Australia is called Tasmania.
5. F Hawaii's highest elevation is Mt. Mauna Kea.
6. T
7. F New Zealand consists of two islands.
8. T
9. T
10. F Cape Horn is on the southern tip of South Africa. The Cape of Good Hope is on the southern tip of South America.

Where in the World? **Page 52**

1. first European to sail around the Cape of Good Hope, 1487-1488
2. Arabia and Eastern Africa; reached Lake Tanganyika, 1853-1858.
3. North Mississippi River region with Jacques Marquette, 1673
4. flew over North Pole1926; 1929 flew over South Pole
5. led U.S. Navy submarine under Arctic waters to North Pole, 1958
6. crossed Rocky Mountains to Pacifc Ocean with Meriwether Lewis,
7. Great Lakes area and tracked Mississippi River to Gulf of Mexico, 1679-1682
8. east-central Africa, 1878-1892
9. Afghanistan, West India, 331 B.C., 326 B.C.
10. first European to reach mainland North America, 1000

Ship Ahoy! **Page 53**

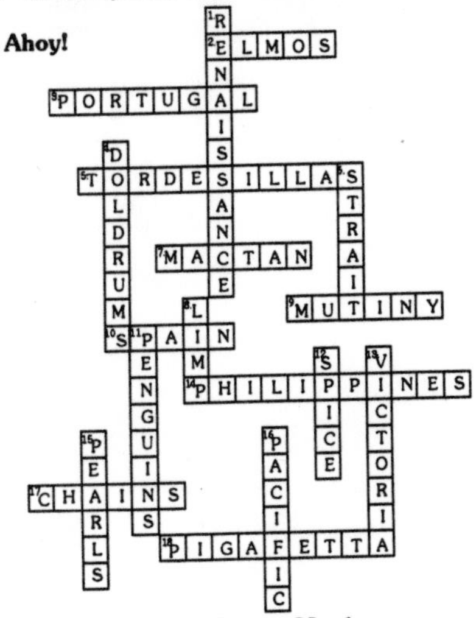

Henry Hudson

The Highlights of Henry Hudson **Page 58**

1. b	5. c
2. a	6. c
3. a	7. a
4. b	8. b

Hudson's History **Page 60**

1. As temperature decreases, molecules in water move slower and pull together to line up in rows. This forms ice. When chunks of ice break away from a glacier and flow into the water, the sun and wind wear down the top of the iceberg. The bottom melts more slowly so it is larger than what can be seen above. (That is why they are very dangerous to ships.)
2. A guilder is the monetary unit used in the Netherlands. One guilder is equal to about 52 cents in American money.
3. Spices were used not only to flavor food but to preserve meats. People did not bathe regularly, so spices were used in creating perfumes and oils. These scents helped people smell better!
4. Sebastian Cabot was a British explorer in the 1500s who searched for a passage to China. He sailed to North and South America. His first expedition was in 1497. Cabot also helped to form the Muscovy Company.

Sail On **Page 61**

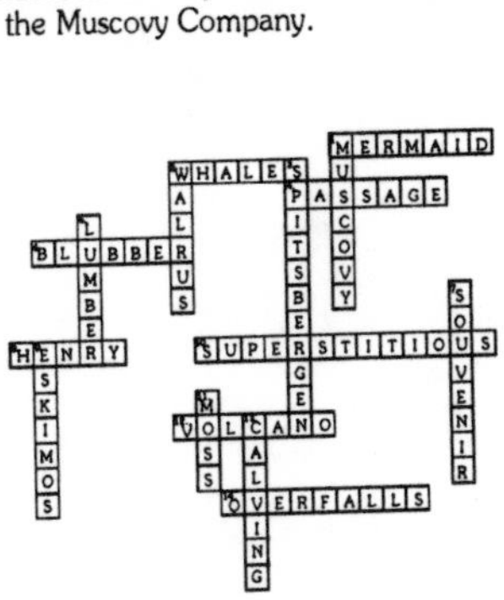

North Country **Page 62**

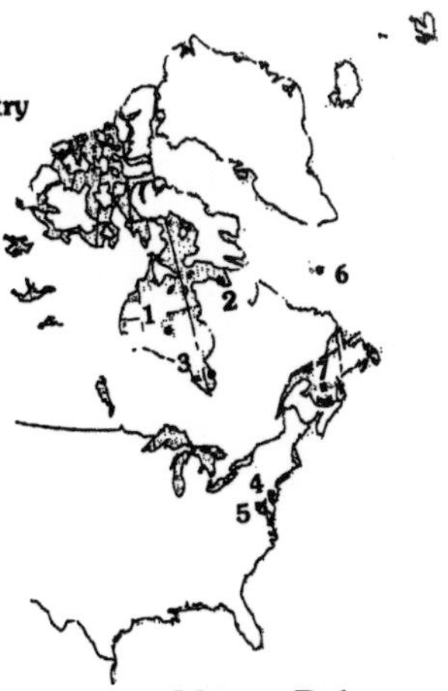

Marco Polo

Voyage to the Orient **Page 67**

1. c	5. a
2. b	6. b
3. c	7. b
4. a	8. a

Travel to Cathay **Page 68**

1. F Beijing is the capital of China.
2. T
3. F The sea north of Taiwan is the East China Sea.
4. T
5. F China borders 11 other countries.
6. T
7. F The country west of 80°E is Iran (formerly Persia).
8. T
9. F The Gulf of Tonkin borders both China and Vietnam.
10. T

Marco's Journey **Page 69**

1. Fuel, heat, and oxygen will create a fire. At higher elevations, oxygen is less plentiful than at lower elevations, so fires do not burn well.
2. Confucianism teaches a respect for ancestors and for the past. It is based on beliefs of Confucius, a Chinese philosopher born around 550 B.C. In this religion, parents rule children, men rule women, and ceremony and duty are very important.
   Taoism is a reaction against Confucianism. Taoism teaches people to live simply in harmony and nature. Taoists meditate, believe in magic, and recite scriptures. Buddhism teaches tha there is a continuing cycle of death and rebirth. Buddhists believe each person's behavior determines his or her role in the next life.
3. Genghis Khan was a Mongolian conqueror who ruled the largest land empire in the history of the world. Considered a military genius, he was harsh and strict with discipline to create a strong army. He ruled Mongolia and invaded China and then central Asia. His grandson was Kublai Khan.

Description of the World **Page 70**

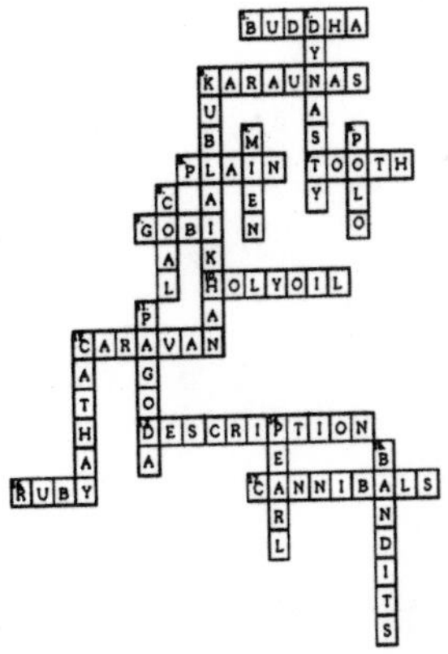

Eastward Ho! **Page 71**

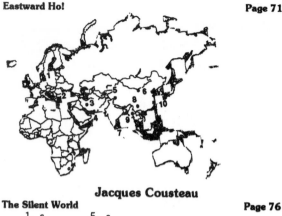

Jacques Cousteau

The Silent World **Page 76**

1. c		5. c
2. c		6. b
3. a		7. a
4. b		8. b

Explore the Depths Below **Page 77**

1. Sonar (*Sound Navigation And Ranging*) is a device that transmits high frequency sound waves through water. If these sound waves or ultrasonic vibrations, strike an object, the beam of vibration is reflected. By calculating the speed of sound through the water, naval scientists can tell how far away an object is.
2. Driftnets are nonbiodegradable nylon plastic nets that can be 50 miles long. They form an invisible curtain which kills mammals, turtles, and seabirds. Hundreds of miles of driftnets have been lost or left in the ocean, trapping marine life.
3. In 1943, Cousteau designed the Aqua-Lung and used it to dive in the Mediterranean. In 1962, Conshelf I was the first underwater habitat. Two men lived for seven days at 33 feet deep. Conshelf II in 1963, held five men for a month at 36 feet and two men were at 90 feet for a week. The US Navy had their first underwater habitat, Sealab I in 1964 aind in 1965 Conshelf III went to 328 feet in the Mediterranean. Dr. Sylvia Earle dived to 1,250 feet off of Oahu, Hawaii in 1979.

Underwater Wonders **Page 78**

1. d		6. a
2. e		7. j
3. g		8. h
4. f		9. b
5. i		10. c

Ocean Geology **Page 80**

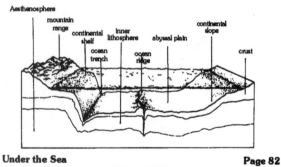

Under the Sea **Page 82**

Charles Darwin

Darwin's Legacy **Page 87**

1. b		5. b
2. c		6. a
3. a		7. c
4. c		8. b

The Natural Naturalist **Page 88**

1. When Darwin was to become a doctor, he couldn't stand the sight of blood and suffering. He was upset with slavery in Brazel and he felt sorry for the South American Indians since the Spanish were destroying their lives. He felt bad for the miners' poor working conditions in Tierra del Fuego and for the cruelty New Zealand slaves had to endure. He sympathized with the Aborigines of Australia.
2. Coral is made from million of polpys which are tiny sea animals. When these animals die, their colorful limestone skeletons form barriers called coral reefs.
3. The lasso is a thin braided leather rope with a loop at one end. Bolas (balls) are two or three leather-covered round rocks joined together with a strap. the gauchos used these to rope cattle.

Which Animals Live Where? **Page 91**

1. e		6. f
2. a		7. b
3. g		8. b
4. a		9. c
5. d		10. d

Survival of the Fittest **Page 92**

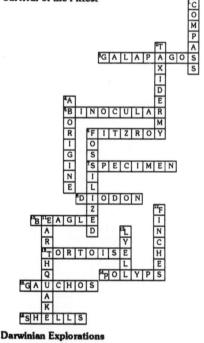

Darwinian Explorations **Page 93**

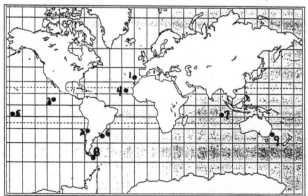

© Frank Schaffer Publications, Inc.

108

FS10131 Explorers